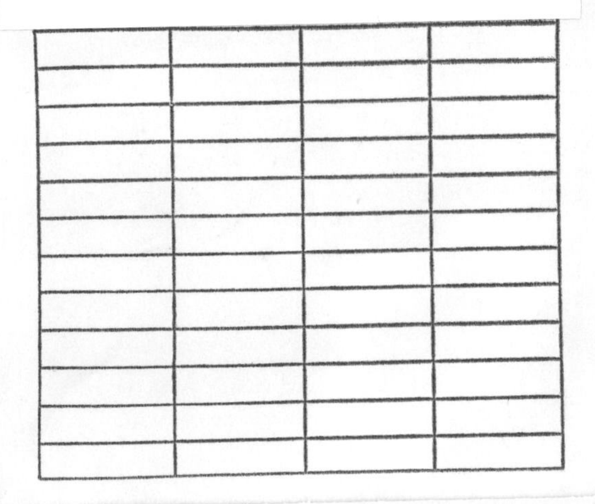

THE COMMUNITY COLLEGE AS AMERICAN THERMOMETER

CLIFFORD ADELMAN

SENIOR ASSOCIATE, OFFICE OF RESEARCH
U.S. DEPARTMENT OF EDUCATION

U.S. Department of Education
Lamar Alexander
Secretary

Office of Educational Research and Improvement
Diane Ravitch
Assistant Secretary

Office of Research
Milton Goldberg
Director

February 1992

For sale by the U.S. Government Printing Office
Superintendent of Documents, Mail Stop: SSOP, Washington, DC 20402-9328
ISBN 0-16-036105-2

Contents

Acknowledgments

Primary thanks are always due my two colleagues, Nabeel Alsalam and Paula Knepper, of the National Center for Education Statistics, for teaching me how to deal with these data, for their own exemplary work with the NLS-72, and for their reviews of earlier versions of this monograph.

Over the past decade, I have learned much about community colleges from Alexander Astin of UCLA, Arthur Cohen of the ERIC Clearinghouse on Community and Junior College at UCLA, Judith Eaton of the American Council on Education, Jim Palmer of the Center for Community College Education at George Mason University, and Jim Ratcliff of Penn State. They have poked, prodded, argued, and questioned. While they may not agree with it, I hope this piece is worthy of their cumulative encouragement.

The Way We Are:
The Community College as American Thermometer

Executive Summary

[This is the third* in a series of monographs based on the data archives of the National Longitudinal Study of the High School Class of 1972 (NLS-72), which has followed a generation of Americans from the time they were seniors in high school into their early thirties. The Base Year (1972) Survey sample consisted of 22,652 students for whom high school records and test scores were also recorded. Followup surveys were conducted in 1973, 1974, 1976, 1979, and 1986. The postsecondary transcripts** of 12,599 individuals in the sample who attended any kind of school or college at any time between 1972 and 1984 are also included in the archives.]

This study looks at a large group of individuals in NLS-72 who enrolled in community colleges at any time between 1972, when they graduated from high school, and 1984, when they were 30 or 31 years old. Some enrolled in community college for a course or two, some for an Associate's degree, some while attending a 4-year college, some after earning a Bachelor's degree. The range is considerable. One out of every four 1972 high school graduates earned at least one credit from a community college over the next 12 years.

By asking who these people were, how they used the community college, and what happened to them in economic life, this study describes the role of this institution in the life of a generation. But the study goes beyond description to demonstrate that the way we are as a learning society is best understood by the way we use community colleges.

By comparing those who enrolled in community colleges to (1) those who enrolled in other kinds of postsecondary institutions, and (2) those whose formal education (at least through 1984) ended in the high school graduation line, this study concludes that:

1. The community college functioned in a variety of "occasional" roles in the lives of individuals. It accommodated their decisions to engage in learning on their own terms, and in their own time. Even if students were constrained by poor academic preparation or economic circumstances, they seemed to make of the community college what they wanted to

---

* The others, along with their U.S. Government Printing Office stock numbers, are: *Light and Shadows on College Athletes* (1990), #065-000-00348-1; and *Women at Thirtysomething: Paradoxes of Attainment* (1991), #065-000-00451-8. They are available, at very modest cost, from the Superintendent of Documents, Washington, D.C. 20402-3238. Phone: (202) 783-3238.

** For those interested in the complete transcript data, *A College Course Map*, GPO stock #065-000-00432-1, is also available from the Superintendent of Documents.

make of it. They used the institution for a time, and then moved on. Some came back. In some respects, these patterns are similar to the ways we use other normative institutions in our society, such as those of religion and the arts.

2. The population using community colleges was more representative of the Class of '72 than those who either did not continue their education at all or who continued it only at 4-year colleges. For minority students (principally Hispanics), students from low and (particularly) moderate socioeconomic backgrounds, students who served in the military, students from the mid-ranks of their high school classes, and students from the lower and mid-ranks of the SAT/ACT population, the percentages attending community colleges were all higher than in the groups not continuing their education or continuing at 4-year colleges. In many ways, those who attend community colleges are more typical of young adults in the U.S. than any other population. They are the average.

3. The community college played a small role in credentialling this generation. The Associate's degree was a weak force: very few people knew what it was or planned to get it; and only 20% of community college attendees actually earned it over 12 years. At the same time, though, the curricula pursued by the mass of community college students indicate that they were more interested in learning or testing their tolerance for higher education than in degrees. Most of them took groups of courses that could be defined in terms of perceived utility on the job or that, in effect, completed their secondary school education.

4. There were no clear cut occupational outcomes of community college attendance. The paths leading from schooling to work were not always linear (attending a 4-year college didn't straighten the line any more than attending a 2-year college). It was also obvious that the occupational aspirations of youth exceeded the realities of age no matter where people went to school or what degree they earned (if any).

5. But earning a degree of <u>any</u> kind, A.A. or B.A., still made a difference: a higher percentage of community college students who earned the A.A. degree, for example, wound up in professional jobs than did 4-year college students who failed to earn the B.A. In fact, some patterns of community college attendance were associated with higher earnings and rates of home ownership than other patterns of postsecondary attendance. But overall, the only pattern of attendance that consistently overcame initial economic circumstance involved a 4-year institution, whether or not a degree was earned.

The Way We Are:
The Community College as American Thermometer

Introduction

Three decades ago, as the distinctive American phenomenon then known as the "junior college" was on the verge of transformation as a type of organization, Burton Clark offered a challenging criticism of its role in our society (Clark, 1960a; 1960b). In his analysis, the junior college played a "cooling out" function. That is, it took whoever entered its doors and tracked them out of the mainstream of social mobility in the United States. It froze their ambitions. It chilled their minds. It iced them with remedial courses. It cut them off from the economic benefits of a society that paid well not only for a Bachelor's degree but for a Bachelor's degree from the right schools that provided the right connections. In an era when those schools and connections meant more than they do today, the junior college was a backwater that reflected but dimly the mission of higher education, and offered, more dimly still, the promise of upward mobility. This happened not by the design of junior college administrators and trustees, but as a by-product of the higher education system. My hyperbolic description of Clark's work notwithstanding, and even though the analysis was drawn from a study of a single junior college in California, Clark was very insightful and credible at the time.

When the Higher Education Act was passed in 1965, there were 654 2-year colleges in the United States, 30% of the total number of institutions of higher education. Two decades later, there were 1,350 2-year colleges, constituting 40% of all institutions of higher education. Very few were called "junior colleges" any more. In 1965, these institutions enrolled 20% of all students at all levels of higher education, including graduate and professional school, and 24% of all first-time college freshmen. Two decades later, the figures were 37% and 44%, respectively (Snyder, 1989). These are official approximate numbers. When a type of institution grows that rapidly in a specific economy or market, its identity and role are likely to change. The climate may even become somewhat warmer. The people who attend may, in fact, define the mainstream.

Most of the growth in the community college sector of U.S. higher education took place in the first decade following passage of the Higher Education Act. The subjects of this monograph, members of the high school class of 1972, graduated from high school toward the end of this steep trajectory. Their use and experience of the community college over the following decade, I propose, can serve as a thermometer of what this institution has become, can tell us, indeed, whether Clark's temperature reading still holds. And to the extent to which people from the Class of '72 who attended community colleges are representative of the Class as a whole, their experience may be emblematic of the ways in which we Americans use other normative institutions such as those of religion and the arts. If so, the accounts laid forth in this study may say much about the way we are.

I. The Question and the Method

This study asks a series of questions about a large group of individuals who associated themselves with a particular type of educational institution, and, through that association, about the role of that institution in our culture. To be sure, this is a limited definition of institutional role. It does not account for the service roles these institutions play in local communities, the economic roles they play in regional labor markets, or the faculties, finances, and governance that influence and shape these other roles (in the matter of community colleges, Breneman and Nelson, 1981). And despite appearances, this definition precludes precise measurements of the economic efficiency of community colleges (Nunley and Breneman, 1988).

Despite appearances, too, this approach to the role of community colleges is not framed in terms of arguments (deriving from Clark's "cooling out" thesis) over whether they promote or hinder access to higher education, whether their principal role is to prepare students for transfer to 4-year colleges, or whether they act as self-interested institutions more than responsive institutions (Folger, H. Astin, and Bayer, 1970; Karabel, 1972; Alba and Lavin, 1981; Cohen and Brawer, 1982; Grubb, 1988; Richardson,1988; Brint and Karabel, 1989) These issues will inevitably arise, but only after we read the record.

The problem with the traditional arguments about the role of the community college is that they subordinate the experience of individuals to larger constructs of social class and status or economic power. These arguments assume that our lives are characterized by order and continuity, and that whatever happens to us has a clear origin, hence an absolute cause. Details, differences, disorder, and discontinuities are not part of this structuralism, and are often swept under the rug. The possibility that individuals and groups can use institutions in the course of making their own history is not admissible. The possibility that patterns and textures of human experience could tell us more than origins and causes is unthinkable to those for whom the superstructures of class and status are all powerful.

But what if an archaeologist of the 25th century stumbled upon the ancient binary remains of the National Longitudinal Study of the High School Class of 1972 (NLS-72)? This massive archive followed a single generation for 14 years with detailed surveys, included high school records and test scores, and, most importantly, gathered the college transcripts of those who attended any kind of postsecondary institution between 1972 and 1984. Watching individuals leave their traces on this archive over and over again, like a palimpsest, what could that archaeologist say about the community college as an institution? And what could that person say about people who attended community colleges, and the patterns and textures of their relationship to the institution? Indeed, patterns and textures govern this account, not superstructures, despite the socioeconomic vocabulary of "earnings," "occupation," and "educational attainment" that are built into government-sponsored surveys such as those of NLS-72.

The record the archaeologist would discover, of course, is hardly complete. One of the principal artifacts on which I rely, a transcript, contains limited information about what students do in an institution. The transcript does not record extra-curricular activities or non-intellective aspects of maturation that we all hope result from participation in postsecondary education. In this case, transcripts also tell us little about the environment of community colleges (see London, 1978), changing attitudes of community college students (see deArmas & McDavis, 1981), the commitments community college students make to their institutions (Stage, 1988), or student involvement that Astin (1984) defined as the amount and quality of effort students devote to learning—all of which influence student progress and attainment to various degrees.

In these contexts, however, and provided they are accurate,[1] transcripts provide a strong link between the circumstances of individuals and groups prior to postsecondary education and their circumstances, activities, and attitudes after postsecondary education. Not cause, but link. They reflect, too, the links between individual choice behavior and both the constraints and possibilities of the institution. The NLS-72 Postsecondary Education Transcript Sample (hereafter referred to as NLS/PETS) provides stronger links in this regard because it covers 12 years of student history and can trace students across state lines and across temporal gaps in attendance. Studies confined to individual institutions or state systems and for shorter periods of time (e.g., Alba and Lavin, 1981) cannot do this.

Others have used the NLS-72 surveys to analyze the careers of community college students (e.g., Breneman and Nelson, 1981; Anderson, 1981; Velez, 1985; Pascarella, 1986; Nunley and Breneman, 1988), or to understand who attends community colleges within the first 2 years of high school graduation (Alexander, Holupka, and Pallas, 1987). But the difference between the survey and transcript data is so significant as to call such analyses into question. For example, Cohen (1988) says that only 825 NLS-72 students enrolled directly in community colleges following high school graduation. Tinto (1987) says 815, Velez and Javalgi (1987) say 1,407, and Grubb (1991)—who presumably used the transcripts—never says.[2] I tried to figure out where these figures came from in the survey data, and gave up. The cleaned NLS/PETS transcripts, on the other hand, show 2,867 students enrolling in community colleges at any time in 1972 (and 2,426 in September alone), the year they graduated from high school. The differences in these figures are too great for comfort. Transcripts may be difficult to interpret at times and occasionally are missing key pieces of data, but they neither exaggerate nor forget.

- Who used the community college?

- When (at what distance from high school graduation, for how long, in relation to attendance at other types of postsecondary institutions)?

- What did they study?

- What credentials did they earn both from the community college and other institutions (and when)?

- What happened to them in the labor market?

These are the basic questions of the data into which we are about to plunge.

To make full sense of these questions, it is important to include in the analysis those who did not continue their education at all after high school. Unlike the other monographs in this collection,[3] then, let alone studies produced on both sides of the "cooling out" debate, this study pays attention to what journalistic shorthand calls "non-college youth."

II. The Story Told by These Data

Let's swim through the data, take the temperature readings, then step back and ask what those readings say about the way we are.

Demographics and Attendance Patterns

The question, "Who attends community colleges in our society?"—like the question, "Who goes to church or to museums?"—is not so simple. The question of who attends cannot be divorced from an understanding of how they attend, and I have rarely met a study that addressed this issue in any terms other than full-time/part-time or completed/dropped out.

Because they cover 12 years of the life of a generation, the postsecondary transcripts of NLS/PETS teach us that there are at least two other ways of describing attendance patterns. The first includes only those people who continued their education after high school, and uses community colleges as the principal reference point. Let's call this framework, the Community College Attendance Pattern.

The second encompasses all students who were seniors in high school in the spring of 1972, and uses credentials earned as its principal reference point. For convenience, let's call this second framework the General Postsecondary Attendance Pattern.

The Community College Attendance Pattern

For purposes of understanding how people attended community colleges, I used a "cascading" logic involving credits earned at different types of institutions, degrees (Associate's and Bachelor's) earned, dates of degrees, and dates of first and last attendance.[4] This logic yielded 10 attendance patterns. For the 12,332 students in the sample whose postsecondary transcript records indicated any earned credits, these patterns are (percentages of students in each category are weighted[5]):

1. Transfer with two degrees. 3.4%
   Students in this group earned both an Associate's degree from a community college and a Bachelor's degree from another kind of institution (4-year college, theological school, 4-year technical college, school of art or design, etc.), and earned the Associate's degree before the Bachelor's. The small number of students who earned

the Associate's degree _after_ the Bachelor's are in category #10. Students who earned Associate's degrees from 4-year colleges are also in category #10.

2. Transfer With One Degree, the Bachelor's. 3.3%
Students in this group earned more than 10 credits from a community college but no Associate's degree, and a Bachelor's degree from a 4-year college. They also attended the community college prior to receiving the BA.

3. Transfer With One Degree, the Associate's. 1.7%
Students in this group earned an Associate's degree from a community college, and more than 10 credits from a 4-year college, but did not complete the Bachelor's degree.

4. Terminal Associate's Degree. 5.7%
Students in this category earned an Associate's degree from a community college. The few who also attended a 4-year college (prior, concurrent, or subsequently), earned 10 or fewer credits from that type of institution, that is, at best, they were "incidental" 4-year college students.

5. No Degree, 2-Year and 4-Year, Non-Incidental. 2.7%
Students in this category attended both community colleges and 4-year institutions, earned more than 10 credits from each type, but never earned any degree, Associate's or Bachelor's. They were "non-incidental" attendees at _both_ types of institutions.

   Slightly more than half of these students attended the community college before enrolling in a 4-year institution, and, technically, are also "transfer" students. The balance are known in the community college literature as "reverse transfers," that is, they entered the 4-year college first and subsequently enrolled in a 2-year college.

6. No Degree, Non-Incidental, 2-Year Only. 15.6%
Students in this category earned more than 10 credits from a community college, but no AA or BA degree. If they also attended a 4-year college, they earned 10 or fewer credits from that institution, that is, they were "non-incidental" attendees at community colleges and "incidental" 4-year college students.

7. No Degree, Incidental, 2-Year. 7.6%
Students in this category earned 10 or fewer credits from a community college, and no degree. Only 4% of them attended other kinds of institutions as well, but also earned 10 or fewer credits from those institutions.

8. No Community College, but 4-Year College. 49.3%
This large slice of the NLS/PETS sample consists of students who attended only 4-year colleges. Within this group, there are six other patterns of attendance and degree attainment. But since none of them refer to the community college, they need not be elaborated here.[6]

9. No Community College, No 4-Year College. 6.7%
Ninety-six percent of the students in this category attended proprietary trade schools, Area Vocational-Technical Institutes or specialized institutions such as hospital schools of nursing, radiologic technology, etc.

10. Other Patterns. 4.1%
This is a residual category for cases that do not fit in the previous nine categories. Some students in this category, for example, earned Associate's degrees from institutions other than community colleges, and may also have earned Bachelor's degrees. Some earned Bachelor's degrees but took a course or two at a community college—either before or after the degree. Some are missing transcript data (credits, grades, dates of attendance, etc.) that might have placed them elsewhere.

The reader will notice the implicit definition of "transfer" in the logic of this first set of attendance patterns. It is a restricted definition with two components: an earned degree (Associate's, Bachelor's or both) and an earned credit threshold (more than 10). I have previously used the "more than 10 credit" threshold (Adelman, 1990a, 1990b, 1991) to describe those who made a commitment to postsecondary education of at least one semester or its equivalent over a period of 12 years. The threshold was derived from analyses of credit production for the entire NLS/PETS sample, and is applied to commitment at any one type of institution. Under this definition, it is insufficient merely to enroll: you have to make a go of it. A transfer is thus not a transfer unless a sufficient (non-incidental) commitment was made to both types of institutions.

If this definition of "transfer" was loosened by not requiring earned degrees, then some students in the 5th attendance pattern ("No Degree, 2-Year and 4-Year, Non-Incidental") would be included, namely those who entered the community college before they enrolled in a 4-year college.

Comparing the restricted and loosened definitions of "transfer," we find the following total percentage of NLS/PETS students transferring over 12 years:

Universe:	Transfer: restricted	Transfer: loosened
All NLS/PETS (12,599)	8.1%	9.5%
Community college attendees (5,708)	18.9	22.2
Attendees earning more than 10 credits from community colleges (4,115)	25.3	29.5

While transfer is a major concern of the literature and ideology of community colleges, "transfer" is treated here as an umbrella term for textures of attendance involving two different types of institutions, textures that (depending on how one defines the universe of students) cover roughly 30% of community college attendees. As the first set of 10 attendance patterns demonstrates, the "transfer" patterns are significant, but hardly exhaustive.

I will refer to these 10 patterns frequently throughout this study and its tables. But they are somewhat difficult to follow—and not always enlightening—when considering questions broader than community college attendance.

General Postsecondary Attendance Patterns

Particularly when comparing the background characteristics and labor market experience of community college students both to 4-year college students and those who did not continue their education after high school, we need a second way of describing attendance patterns: a seven-category configuration, as follows, for the full NLS–72 sample of 22,652 (percentages, as always, are weighted):

1. Transfer With a Bachelor's Degree 3.7%
   Students in this group attended both 2- and 4-year colleges, entering the 2-year college first, and ultimately earning a Bachelor's degree. They may or may not have earned an Associate's degree along the way. Those who didn't, earned more than 10 credits from the 2-year college.

2. Terminal Associate's Degree. 4.2%
   Students in this group earned an Associate's Degree from a community college, but no higher degree. Some 22.7% of the people in this group also earned more than 10 credits from 4-year colleges.

3. No Degree/Non-Incidental. 10.1%
   These students never earned any degree, but attended 2-year colleges where they earned more than 10 credits. Some 14.3% of this group also earned more than 10 credits from 4-year schools.

4. Proprietary/Vocational or Incidental. 7.8%
This category covers students who either attended proprietary/vocational schools only or enrolled in 2-year colleges but earned 10 or fewer credits from those institutions. The rationale for putting these two groups together is that, compared with other groups, they both spent very little time in postsecondary institutions. For example, 65% of the proprietary/vocational school students and 61% of the incidental community college attendees were enrolled for less than 6 months over a 12-year period.

5. Four-Year/Other, With Bachelor's Degree. 19.1%
This category covers those who either attended only 4-year colleges or whose postsecondary attendance patterns are not accounted for by the other patterns but who earned a Bachelor's degree.

6. Four-Year/Other, Without Bachelor's Degree. 11.3%
This category covers students who met the same conditions as in #5, but who did not earn a Bachelor's degree. Some of them earned Associate's degrees from 4-year colleges or specialty schools.

7. None. 43.9%
To the best of our knowledge,[7] these students did not enroll in any kind of postsecondary institution between high school graduation in 1972 and the fall of 1984, when they were 30 or 31 years old.

What do we see in the demographics of the people who continued their education after high school and who fit the various attendance categories described under both the Community College Attendance Pattern and the General Postsecondary Attendance Pattern? The following observations are based on Tables 1 through 4:

- Despite the greater ethnic diversity of the community college student population, blacks from the Class of '72 were far less likely to use the community college in their postsecondary education than Hispanics, and no more likely than whites. This is hardly a new observation (see Alexander, Holupka, and Pallas, 1987; Cohen, 1988). Yet somehow the popular mythology persists that a majority of black college students attend community colleges. That simply was not true for the NLS-72 cohort. Nor does it appear to be true for more recent cohorts (Alsalam and Rodgers, 1991). Observed from a slightly different perspective: of the major minority groups, over time, blacks are the least likely to attend community colleges.

  The reason seems obvious. Some 53% of the black college students in the NLS/PETS sample graduated from high schools in the 17-state southern region (v. 27% of all students in the sample), and most of the Historically Black Colleges (HBCs)—almost all of which are 4-year schools—are in that 17-state region. It has been demonstrated previously (Astin, 1982) that blacks residing in the South prefer to attend HBCs.

- Students from second-language backgrounds exhibited attendance and degree attainment patterns very similar to those for students from English-speaking households. In fact, they were slightly more likely to continue their education after high school (57.5% to 56%).

  These phenomena seem odd for two reasons. First, Hispanics are more likely to attend community colleges than members of other ethnic groups, and, as Table 4 indicates, more than a third of the Hispanics in the PETS sample came from non-English-speaking households.[8] Secondly, among students from second language backgrounds who entered postsecondary education, the proportion from the lowest SES quartile is double what it is among students from English-speaking households. Since community colleges serve a higher percentage of low SES students than do 4-year colleges, we would again expect to find a concentration of second language background students in the community college attendance patterns.

  But among the universe of second-language students in the NLS/PETS, only 18% were Hispanic. Three out of four were either white or Asian-American, and their attendance patterns balance out those of Hispanic students.

- Women who attended community colleges were more likely than men to earn terminal Associate's degrees, and less likely than men to use the community college as a way station on the road to the Bachelor's degree. As previously demonstrated (Adelman, 1991), women in the generation of NLS-72 were less likely than men to continue their education after high school, but among those who did continue, women were more likely than men to earn credentials.

- Community colleges served a higher proportion of NLS-72 students from low and (particularly) medium SES backgrounds than did 4-year colleges, but a lower proportion than did proprietary and trade schools (see Table 3). In fact, in terms of socioeconomic status, it was the medium-range student in the Class of '72 who was most likely to attended a community college.

  However, there is no question that the critical community college attendance categories encompassing "no degree" students and terminal Associate's degree students house a higher proportion of people from low SES backgrounds than do other attendance categories (Table 3).

The basic demography (race, sex, socioeconomic status), then, both challenges and confirms popular mythology. This demography may turn out to be slightly different for the next major group in the U.S. Department of Education's longitudinal studies program, the High School Class of 1982, but in ways that only confirm the basic trends noted above. National surveys of total enrollments (Snyder, 1989) show that, by 1986, a majority of minority college students attended community colleges, but this came about principally from further increases in the percentage of community college students who were Hispanic, a dramatic increase in the percentage of community college students who were Asian-Americans (a group that was too small to disaggregate in the Class of '72), and a corresponding drop in the proportions of both whites and blacks.[9]

Such cross-sectional enrollment surveys, however, tell us nothing about the more important phenomena of attendance patterns—which emerge only over time. We have no idea what kinds of enrollments these may turn out to be. It is for that reason, among others, that we eagerly await the 10-year postsecondary transcript sample for the Class of 1982 (also known as the "High School and Beyond/Sophomore Cohort," the members of which were first surveyed as 10th graders in 1980).

Considered only as a demographic variable, the age at which this cohort attended community college must be inferred from first and last dates of attendance (where known), and assuming an age of 18 in 1972. As Table 5 indicates, well over half the community college attendees had come and gone before they were 22, but 26% (and a slightly higher percentage of women) were enrolled at some time between the ages of 25 and 30.

It may very well be that community colleges serve significant numbers of "older" students, but if so, a large proportion appear to be enrolled in non-credit or continuing education programs. The NLS-72 archive provides survey data on school attendance and status through age 32 (as opposed to age 30 on the transcripts). Some 16.5% of the entire sample indicated enrollment in some kind of school between the ages of 30 and 32 (1984-1986). Of this group, 30% attended community colleges. Of this group, in turn, 39% classified themselves as special students and 31% indicated no degree objectives. Those are large pieces of a small group.

Time of Attendance

The last of the demographic observations leads us to consider the points in their educational careers at which the members of the High School Class of 1972 used the community college.

There are a number of ways to approach the time factor. The first is somewhat limited in coverage but strong as a bench mark: the distribution of Associate's degrees by year of receipt.

Year of associate's degrees earned by high school class of 1972

Year	All	From community colleges	From other types of institutions
		(percent)	
<1974	1.0	1.1	0.8
1974	45.4	44.8	48.2
1975	18.4	18.4	18.2
1976	10.0	10.6	6.8
1977–78	10.7	10.2	13.1
1979–80	7.3	7.6	5.8
1981–84	7.2	7.3	7.2

Approximately three-quarters of those who earned Associate's degrees by 1984, then, did so within 4.5 years of graduation from high school, that is, by the end of 1976. Those who use the community college for purposes of credentialing, it appears, do so at comparatively early points in their lives.

A second way to consider the time spent by students in community colleges is to analyze the gap between dates of first and last enrollment. As Table 6 indicates,

- Incidental attendees (earned 10 or fewer credits) did not take a course one year then come back years later for another course. In other words, whatever they did in a community college, they got it over with quickly. It is not surprising that they were the least likely of all attendance groups to say, at age 26, that they were tired of school.

- Approximately one-third of the non-incidental community college attendees (including AA recipients) were enrolled in community colleges for a period of 40 months or more. That does not mean that they enrolled every semester or that they enrolled full-time. It simply means that the student came back to the institution time and time again. We might call this phenomenon "continuous use."

- Nearly half of those who attended community colleges were enrolled for less than 16 months. Of this group, 30% earned at least 30 credits during that period of time, which is about what one would expect for full-time students; but 40% earned 10 or fewer credits, indicating incidental status.

Taken together, these three patterns indicate that the relationships between most community college students and their institutions were too brief to have much impact beyond the classroom. All the better reason, as we will see, to pay close attention to what people study in community colleges.

A third way to think about the time factor is in terms of the date of entry either to postsecondary education in general (see Table 7) or to community colleges, in particular (see Table 8). As Knepper (1989) has demonstrated, delayed entry does not affect the time it takes to earn a B.A. for those who earn it. But delayed entry does lessen the likelihood that the degree will be earned at all. The NLS/PETS transcript data indicate that, even over a 12-year period, there is a direct correlation between when people enter community colleges and their ultimate educational attainment. In this respect, it bears noting that only among "incidental" community college students do we find a significant percentage who delayed entry to postsecondary education by more than 30 months (see Table 7). For the Class of '72, the later in life one entered a community college, the more incidental one's use of the institution.

In addition, students who were on active military duty at any time between 1972 and 1979 (6.5% of the transcript sample) not only attended community colleges in higher proportions than the entire transcript sample (54.6% v. 42.3%), but also—as one would expect—tended to delay entry to community colleges for 2 years or more after high school graduation, hence were less likely to earn degrees (see Table 9).[10] Among the military personnel, patterns of attendance by race were the same as for the general population: blacks were less likely to use the community college, Hispanics more likely.

Two-thirds of all those who attended community college by the time they were 30 or 31 years old entered postsecondary education (in any kind of institution) directly from high school, and 80% entered within 18 months of high school graduation (Table 7). But that percentage varied with attendance pattern, and in direct relationship to the level of degree(s) earned. This phenomenon suggests that students on the "transfer" tracks had a fairly good idea when they were seniors in high school that they would transfer, hence did not unduly delay postsecondary entry.

Among all high school seniors in the NLS-72 sample, only 9% planned to transfer from one kind of institution to another. But among those who planned to attend 2-year colleges, the proportion with definite or tentative plans to transfer was 53%. And among those who eventually attended 2-year colleges and transferred, the proportion planning to do so as high school seniors was 85%. In general, then, those who plan to transfer—even before they enter higher education—are more likely to do so.

The Role of Aspirations and Plans

Entry to postsecondary education in terms of both time and place involves many choices. Among the conditions and constraints on those choices are the student's own aspirations and plans for further education. Previous analyses invoking the aspirations of NLS-72 students who attended community colleges (e.g., Levin and Clowes, 1980; Velez, 1985; Velez and Javalgi, 1987; Nunley and Breneman, 1988) were concerned principally with the issue of predicting the attainment of the Bachelor's degree, and were based wholly on survey data. But with reference to the transcript data, the distinction between aspirations and plans is complex and revealing, and is presented in Tables 10 and 11.

In the initial questionnaire administered to them as high school seniors, the NLS-72 participants were asked two questions: "What is the highest level of education you would like to attain?" and "What is the highest level of education you plan to attain?" The differences in their responses to those questions are underscored by the actual attainment of this group 12 years later (Table 11), as well as by the percentage in each category of aspiration or plan who entered postsecondary education immediately following high school, that is, who sought to actualize their aspirations or plans as early as possible.[11]

Table 10 presents the differences between aspirations and plans for groups of students by demographic and ability characteristics. As one would expect, there is a continuous down-shifting from aspirations to plans, but the extent and distribution of the shifts are irregular. For example, 54% of all NLS-72 students aspired to the Bachelor's degree (I include both the "4-year college/BA" and the "Graduate school" categories here). This percentage drops to 43% when the terms of the question are plans. Where does the difference go? What did these 11% of the NLS-72 students plan to do when the Bachelor's degree option was removed?

Roughly a quarter of the students in that group shifted their plans to community colleges, but nearly half dropped their plans for postsecondary education altogether. As Table 10 demonstrates, this pattern differs somewhat by race and socioeconomic status:

- Hispanics in the NLS-72 had consistently lower aspirations than either blacks or whites (43% of Hispanics, 52% of blacks, and 55% of whites aspired to the Bachelor's). When the question shifts to plans, Hispanics lowered their targets by a far more significant amount than either blacks or whites.

- With the shift from aspirations to plans, the community college gains among whites and Hispanics, but not as much among blacks. This phenomenon is consistent with the demography of community college attendance noted earlier.

- Only students in the highest SES quartile maintained plans roughly equivalent to aspirations. Their only trade-off was between graduate school and the BA.

The data on aspirations and plans in relation to SAT/ACT scores demonstrates a greater degree of down-shifting among students in the lower bands, indicating that they are not oblivious to their own general learned abilities. [For purposes of these analyses, ACT scores were converted to the SAT scale.] To the extent to which students scoring above 975 refocused from aspirations to plans, on the other hand, the trade-off was largely between graduate school and the Bachelor's degree.

A closer—and different—look at SAT scores in relation to aspirations and plans reinforces the realism of students' self-appraisal:

Mean SAT scores by educational aspirations and plans
(standard deviation in parentheses)

Highest education level	**Aspired**	**Planned**
High school graduate	849 (202)	821 (177)
Voc/trade school	830 (171)	840 (173)
Community college/AA	817 (158)	834 (159)
4-year college/BA	912 (184)	957 (189)
Graduate school	1014 (201)	1049 (212)

In all categories save "high school graduate," the mean scores for the group that planned to attain a given level of education are higher than those for the group that aspired to that level, that is, there is a better match. Where there is a better match between a student's sense of his/her abilities and his/her educational goals, we would like to think that the student will attempt to actualize those goals as soon as possible. If that hypothesis is true, the relationship between educational plans and time of entry into postsecondary education should be direct. Indeed, it is:

Percent of students who entered postsecondary education directly from high school, by educational plans

Highest level planned	All NLS-72 seniors	PETS sample only
Graduate school	73.1	82.4
4-year college/BA	71.5	83.3
Community college/AA	45.9	69.4
Vocational/trade school	19.7	50.8
High school graduate	4.1	27.8

The Weak Force of Credentials

What should be obvious from this presentation so far is that the community college did not loom large in either the aspirations or plans of the NLS-72 high school seniors. Only 12.4% of the entire cohort planned to attend a community college, and only 8.5% of the entire cohort (and 14.2% of those who actually attended postsecondary institutions) planned to earn the Associate's degree (the principal credential awarded by community colleges) as their highest credential. Another 8.2% (and 15.4% of those who actually attended) planned postsecondary vocational or technical education. While it is true that some proprietary and vocational schools award the Associate's degree, the NLS-72 high school seniors knew the difference between a trade school and a community college.[12]

Not only was the bench mark credential of the Associate's degree dimly visible in the plans of the NLS-72 cohort; it was also a weak force. That is, over time, and compared with the Bachelor's degree, very few people who initially planned to get an Associate's degree actually got it—even in 12 years: 26% versus 55% of those who planned to get the Bachelor's and actually received it. Not only that, but 30% of those who initially planned an Associate's degree never attended a community college at all, and another 15% were but incidental attendees.

Community colleges award "certificates" in addition to Associate's degrees. But only 4% of the NLS-72 community college attendees received such certificates. The recipients tended to be white women who did not earn any other credential or degree, and the most common fields for certificates were secretarial (14%) and allied health/nursing (24%).

What's at issue in this discussion is the certifying function of community colleges in the educational career of this cohort. To what extent are Associate's degrees or certificates awarded by community colleges primary goals of students? To what extent are they consolation prizes? Are the credentials relevant at all to the education of a generation? The transcript data strongly suggest that people attend community colleges principally for purposes that have little to do with earning credentials. The credentialing role of the community college is, in fact, a minor aspect of its mission.

Do the ways in which students use community colleges in this respect say more about the way we are than the popular perception of a credential-hungry society? Does our economic life demand credentials—or something else—from education? These are questions worth pondering, but only after we have learned some more from the NLS-72 archive.

Attendees: Academic Background and General Ability

In order to appreciate what the community college does for the people who attend (depending on how and when they attend), it is helpful to consider what those people bring to the community college in terms of previous education. For this task, the NLS-72 archive contains high school records, high school class rank, and a variety of ability measures.

In addition to providing baseline information against which to set community college coursetaking patterns, general educational attainment, and basic labor market outcomes, these academic background variables, in fact, help explain and refine our analysis of community college attendance patterns.

The data on high school class rank (see Table 12), high school curriculum (see Table 13), and equated SAT/ACT scores (see Table 14) present a complex portrait of community college attendees. It is obvious, first, that those who never continued their education after high school had the weakest backgrounds, no matter what measure one uses. Community colleges may be open-door institutions, but there are many high school graduates who aren't prepared to walk through that door—and who, furthermore, aren't interested in walking through.[13] While the gaps between the high school performance (class rank, SAT/ACT scores) of the weakest group of community college students (the incidental attendees) and the NLS-72 seniors who did not enter postsecondary education at all through age 30 are not great, the differences in curricular backgrounds in math, science, and foreign languages are more noticeable.

The few highly talented students in the NLS-72 simply did not attend community colleges, regardless of socioeconomic background. The data on this issue will no doubt surprise many who have contended that "high ability" students from low SES backgrounds are (a) shunted into community colleges and (b) do not earn Bachelor's degrees (Folger, H. Astin, and Bayer, 1970; Karabel, 1972; Brint and Karabel, 1989; Grubb, 1991; ETS, 1991). Part of the problem lies in the definition of "high ability" or "high talent" (Karabel and A. Astin, 1975) or "high resource" (Alexander, Holupka, and Pallas, 1987). Surprisingly, most of these analyses use a single, aggregate measure of ability or talent, and few of them tell us where the "cut-score" for "high" whatever-it-is lies. That's not fair.

The definition of "high academic resource students" used here involves three measurements, each of a different kind. First, we take the top quartile of performers on a special ability test (a mini-SAT) given to most NLS-72 participants as high school seniors. Second, we use high school class rank, and again take the top quartile. Third, we use high school records and draw in anyone who took either more than 5 semesters of math, or more than 5 semesters of science, or more than 5 semesters of foreign languages (that's a fairly flexible formula). A "high academic resource student" must be in all three measurement groups. Only 5% of the entire NLS-72 sample—and 8% of those who continued their education after high school—met all three criteria.

Table 15 lays out who these "high academic resource students" were and what happened to them. It's a small group, particularly when distributed across three SES categories times either seven patterns of attendance or five levels of degree attainment. So the standard errors of measurement are sometimes large, and the comparisons are not always statistically significant. Nonetheless, we can say that the vast majority—nearly 80% of them—never set foot in a community college. Only 7.5% of the entire group of "high academic resource" students came from the lowest socioeconomic quartile—versus 53.8% from the highest SES quartile—and the principal sorting criterion was not the ability test, but the curricular thresholds. No matter how generous the formula, the results demonstrate that low SES students are far less likely then others to take one of the three major elective pieces of a college preparatory curriculum in high school.

What distinguishes all the low SES and high SES groups here is whether they continued their education after high school at all, not where they went to school or what degrees they earned. Some 13% of the high academic resource/low SES students—versus about 6% of the high academic resource/high SES students—did not enter any kind of postsecondary institution by the time they were 30 years old. That turns out to be a statistically significant difference. Of those who continued their education (NLS/PETS), some 72% of the high academic resource/low SES students earned at least a Bachelor's degree versus 80% of the high academic resource/high SES students. That turns out not to be a statistically significant difference. In other words, there was no difference in the Bachelor's degree achievement rate of low SES and high SES students of similarly strong academic preparation and ability!

For the entire NLS-72 sample, those who eventually earned degrees of <u>any</u> kind brought a stronger background to postsecondary education than those who didn't, and that is no surprise. A higher percentage of transfer students who eventually earned Bachelor's degrees took requisite college preparatory curricula in math and science than did students who attended only 4-year colleges and never earned a Bachelor's degree. Those who earned terminal Associate's degrees brought higher SAT/ACT scores, class ranks, and science and foreign language backgrounds to the community college than the non-incidental students who failed to earn an Associate's degree.

Failure to earn a degree, however, was due neither to poor academic performance in the community college, nor, as Karabel (1972) darkly hinted, to a plot by community colleges to flunk out unpromising "transfer track" students: no one who earned 30 or more credits from a community college but no degree had a GPA less than "C." And since only 9% of community college course enrollments wind up as "Incompletes" or "Withdrawals" (versus 11% for research universities, 12% for comprehensive colleges, and 14% for liberal arts colleges), it is highly unlikely that this group failed to earn degrees due to failure to complete courses and receive a grade (even an "F").

Since the "no degree" attendance patterns cover the largest group of community college attendees, since the time-frame for completion was 12 years (a rather substantial period), and since common sense would indicate that lack of financial aid is not a major cause of withdrawal from low-cost, open-door commuter institutions, we ought to advance some other hypotheses as to why they did not finish a degree program.

This inquiry will take us directly into the curricular experience of community college students. I propose that there are two distinct curricular patterns of those who attend community colleges, but earn no degree whatsoever.

The first—and involving the largest group (about 75%)—is a pattern of coursework with no distinct focus. Grubb (1991) calls this phenomenon "milling around." While for some, "milling around" constitutes a *de facto* completion of high school, for others there is no such goal. And when there are no goals, it is easier to disengage.

The second curricular pattern involves a sufficiently distinct course of study (usually occupational in nature) for students to take from that curricular experience what they think they need for the labor market. The formal credential is not a concern; the subject matter is. Goals apply here, but they can be stated in terms of "sufficient knowledge." If this hypothesis holds, it will reinforce my previous contention that the credentialing function of the community college is not one of its principal missions, and that the way we are has more to do with learning than with pieces of paper.

Indeed, the NLS-72 students who attended community college demonstrate that learning without the currency of credentials drives us more than we think. While that learning may not pay off as much as the credential (as we shall see), it appears to drive us nonetheless.

Coursetaking: The Community College as Provider of Knowledge

Let us follow up this notion, first, by examining Table 16. The table compares the "majors" of those who received an Associate's degree from a community college with those of students who never earned any degree but who did earn at least a year's worth of credits from a community college. The Associate's degree completers obviously include a large percentage (43%) who "majored" in general studies or traditional arts and sciences subjects. Given the fact that 30% of the completers transferred to 4-year institutions <u>and</u> eventually earned a B.A., and that the general studies or traditional arts and sciences curricula are more likely to lead to B.A.s,[14] that 43% is in line with expectations.

In examining hundreds of individual records of "no degree" students who earned 30 or more credits in community colleges, however, I could determine a concentration (defined as either a minimum of 15 credits in a single field or allied fields, or two-thirds of credits in traditional arts and sciences curricula) for 66% of them. Of this group, about a fourth "majored" in traditional arts and sciences subjects. Among the rest, courses of study were dominated by occupational fields for which no license or degree is required, for example, business administration, engineering technologies, office support occupations.

The tendency to take from the community college that knowledge of immediate use in the workplace—and without regard to credentials—is illuminated by Table 17, which answers the following question: How much more likely were NLS/PETS students to take a particular course within an attendance pattern largely limited to community colleges versus an attendance pattern involving both community colleges and 4-year colleges? To illustrate the reading of Table 17: a student who attended community colleges in either an incidental, no degree, or terminal Associate's degree pattern is roughly 4 times as likely to have taken "Technical Mathematics" as a transfer student.

The list of courses with high ratios in Table 17 is dominated by subjects of either just such workplace utility (Technical Drafting, Data Processing, Office Machines), or pre-collegiate courses in math and English (which are prerequisites to everything else), or courses in the standard curricula of Nursing (Anatomy and Physiology, General Health Sciences), or the Police Academy (General Law Enforcement). In the latter connection, let us remember that the period during which the NLS-72 cohort went to college was one in which institutions of higher education received "Capitation Grants" for nursing students, and the Law Enforcement Assistance Act provided plentiful funding of postsecondary police training. Those occupational training support systems are no longer as generous.

But asking what courses one is "more likely" to take under a given community college attendance pattern produces a different answer from the question of what courses yield the highest percentage of credits earned. Credits are proxy measures for time; and Table 18 presents the courses accounting for the highest percentage of total time spent in higher education by students who attended community colleges. Again, I have split the list according to community college attendance pattern. The 43 courses in the left-hand column of Table 18 account for 48.3% of the all credits (hence, all postsecondary time) of those who attended community colleges as either incidental, no degree, or terminal Associate's degree students. The 43 courses in the right-hand column, on the other hand, account for 43.8% of the credits (hence, time) of all those who attended community colleges in patterns involving 4-year college attendance.

Let us note, first, the degree of concentration in the curricular experience of this generation. That only 43 course categories (out of 969 in which community college enrollments were recorded) account for such a large proportion of the total time spent in higher education by community college attendees indicates that those students followed fairly narrow paths through the offerings of the institution. As a guide to interpretation, the median percentage of credits generated by any one course category was less than 0.15%. So to observe a course such as Computer Programming or Medical/Surgical Nursing generating 0.5% of all credits is to observe a significant cut of the postsecondary time of this category of students.

Second, there is a substantial overlap in the two lists of courses: 29 out of 43 appear on both lists (though in slightly different order). The characteristics of the 14 cases for which the lists differ follow from the academic backgrounds of students in the two blocks of attendance patterns, as well as from our previous notion of "workplace utility":

Community College Only	Community and 4-Year College
Nursing: Medical/Surgical	English Literature
Stenography	Developmental Psychology
Secretarial: General	American Literature
Automotive Mechanics	Organic Chemistry
Clerk-Typist	Statistics (Math)
Intro. to Business Admin.	Physical Science: General
Introductory College Math	Philosophy: General, Introduction
Business Math: Arithmetic	Zoology: General, Introduction
Technical Math	Elementary or Intermediate French
Personal Health: General	Physical Education (Education)
Electronics Technology	Bible Studies
Remedial Reading	Geography: Introduction
Data Processing	Finance
Computer Programming	Geology: General

Given the comparatively weak secondary school mathematics background of community college attendees in the no-degree and terminal-Associate's categories (see Table 13), it is not surprising to see the heavy representation of pre-collegiate mathematics in their curricular experience. Community college programs for this generation evidently insisted on both remediation and on mathematics prerequisites for their major occupationally oriented programs.

The 29 courses that appear on both lists, though, are principally introductions to the basic arts and sciences disciplines. In that respect, the community college also seemed to insist on providing at least the rudiments of a general education to a far larger proportion of its students than merely to those who transferred.

The Concept of "Principal Provider"

This presentation of curricular experience raises the question of what type of institution was the "principal provider" of a given curricular content to this generation of students. The question is important from a labor market perspective because if we assume that the knowledge-content of work is determined by the learning people bring to the workplace, we can (a) identify those dysfunctions in work force preparedness that can be traced to prior education, hence, target our educational improvement efforts more precisely, and (b) better match exiting college and community college students to the labor market by referring to what they studied. If we need X, we will know better which type of institution is the principal provider; and if we need a better X, we will know which provider to target for improvement efforts.

Of what kinds of knowledge, within fields, is the community college the principal provider to our economy and society?

Table 19 attempts to explore an approach to this question through the concept of enrollment differentials. It takes some illustrative fields, and selects, from within those fields, courses typically offered by both 2-year and 4-year colleges in which total enrollments were dominated by the community college. For each course, a contrasting case is offered: another course in that general field for which the community college is not the principal provider. For example, if one were looking for a technical writer, one would more likely turn to the universe of community college students than one would if the job involved creative writing. Likewise for real estate agents as opposed to insurance agents; child care specialists as opposed to family relations counselors, and so forth.

Not all courses, to be sure, are so occupationally specific. Some, however, are tied to occupational curricula, for example, the Engineering Physics course to the Engineering Technologies programs offered in community colleges versus the Engineering Mechanics course frequently taken by Engineering majors in 4-year colleges. But within traditional arts and sciences courses, the community college is a principal player only at the introductory/general level. There is nothing wrong with this: for most of us, the knowledge received through formal education in all areas, save our specialization, is general and introductory. It's part of the way we are.

Labor Market Outcomes: the Emphases of Work

What happened in the labor market to those students from the High School Class of 1972 who attended community colleges? Given the very rich data on the 5th (1986) follow-up survey of the NLS-72, there are many ways to approach the question, and many labor market variables upon which we can draw (earnings, unemployment, industry, etc.) At this point in the discussion, however, I want to focus on two connections between curricular experience and work.

First, let us note the general distribution of occupations held by NLS-72 community college attendees in 1986, presented by attendance pattern (Table 20). "Occupation," to be sure, is not a very informative category of analysis, since what people actually do on the job is more important to our understanding of the relationship between education and work than what people call themselves. Nonetheless, and despite the slipperiness of some occupational categories (e.g., "Managers"), Table 20 not only provides some basic parameters, but also lends strength to the analyses above.

The most interesting group in terms of the overall topic of this paper are the terminal Associate's degree holders. Even though credentialing may not be one of the principal roles of the community college, and the Associate's degree a weak force in the aspirations and plans of students, that degree, nonetheless, is the basic credential for the U.S. community college.

Furthermore, we can be sure that people who earned an Associate's degree from a community college experienced as full a range of community college curricula as the bench mark 60-credits allows (though 70.6% of terminal Associate's degree holders earned more than 60 credits from community colleges). In other words, this group had maximum exposure to the principal provider of its postsecondary education, and without major contamination of curricular experience at another type of institution.

For their present or most recent job, the 1986 survey asked NLS-72 respondents the degree to which they worked with ideas, people, paper, and things. Table 21 presents the responses, by major course of study, of Associate's degree recipients (from community colleges) who were in the college transcript sample and who claimed they worked "a great deal" with ideas or people. Most of the responses fit common sense empiricism. On the assumption that they are working in the general area of their community college concentration, majors in "Protective Services" need to work with the law (ideas) as well as people. Those in business support services work far more with people than with ideas. There thus appears to be a general match between curriculum and work role.

In terms of aggregate rankings, respondents worked mostly with people, followed by paper, ideas, and things, with the spread between people and ideas being 21.4%. These aggregate rankings well reflect the overall role of ideas in the community college curriculum.

But what happens if we focus the same questions only on those who said (in the 1986 survey) that they used their postsecondary education a great deal in their work? Within this group, the proportion who said they worked "a great deal" with ideas is 20% higher than that for the entire universe of Associate's degree holders.

What this variation implies is that a community college curriculum dominated by ideas is far more occupationally relevant, has far more actual "workplace utility," than the curriculum experienced by the mass of those who study in community colleges. In fact, the proportion of Associate's degree recipients for whom education was very relevant to work and who worked a great deal with ideas is higher than that for Bachelor's degree recipients who never attended a community college (70% v. 63%).

III. College, Church, Museum: Where Are We?

For the past 20 pages or so we have been swimming through a great deal of data, though perhaps (believe it or not) not enough. What does this account tell us about the role of the community college in the lives of a generation? Much of what we have seen confirms previous analyses or imputations from national databases such as the Current Population Surveys of the Bureau of the Census or the Higher Education General Information Surveys. But the transcript data both augment and depart from previous analyses in ways that encourage us to reconfigure the very language we use to describe the mission of the community college, and in at least two ways.

Occasional Institutions

First, the institution seems to function in a variety of what I would call "occasional" roles. In a more common phrasing, it serves individuals for *ad hoc* purposes. While there are regular church-goers and museum habitues, our uses of those institutions are more likely to resemble attendance patterns at community colleges. An institution capable of an occasional role must be very flexible, tractable, and penetrable. That doesn't mean that the institution is friendly, efficient, or effective. In the case of community colleges, it does not necessarily mean that the institution provides quality instruction or guidance, or that it keeps its promises to students. It simply means that the institution easily accommodates a variety of decisions to engage in intentional learning within a formal organization. Governed by the culture of credentialism and its timetable, 4-year colleges are less accommodating.

The students whose records we see in this archive are adults, and their choices to use a particular institution for a particular purpose at a particular time in their lives are intentional, even if the purpose is "milling around." What the community college does is to canonize and formalize the many decisions we make as adults to engage in learning for either limited, highly focused purposes or for general purposes. The community college is thus neither a "terminal" institution (Karabel, 1972) nor a transfer institution. Beyond the "value" of learning (the normative aspect of its existence), its purpose and role is not so easily fixed (Zwerling, 1986). The same can be said of other institutions, for example, churches and museums, that speak a language of values (the normative), but that serve us in very practical, utilitarian ways.

A second version of this theme (and it is qualitatively different from the first) is that the community college functions as an intermediary institution: a way-station or stepping stone or gap-filler for individuals in transit from one status to another, for example, adolescent student to labor market adult, working adolescent to adult student, etc. The universes of the labor market and baccalaureate education, however complex, have far more definite boundaries, rules, and expectations in the lives of individuals than does the community college. While it is hard to infer student motivation from transcript data, it appears that students in all attendance patterns (including "Incidental") knew that the community college would do something for them, would help them get from here to there. Even if they were constrained by geography, family circumstances, poor academic preparation, or socioeconomic status, they seemed to make of the community college what they wanted to make of it. They used the institution for a time, and then moved on.

A third version of this theme casts the community college in the role of "testing ground." That is, the institution provides individuals with the chance to test their tolerance for and interest in postsecondary education. More than half of those whose educational aspirations as high school seniors were limited to the high school diploma eventually attended community colleges, but a third of those people decided that postsecondary education was not for them, and became incidental students.

These variations on the "occasional use" theme reinforce Grubb's (1988) observation that labor market conditions and anticipated rate-of-return are not powerful factors in motivating students to enroll in community colleges. These variations on occasional use also call into question the very idea of "attrition" or dropping out of community colleges.

From their days as seniors in high school through age 30, the community college functioned in the lives of NLS-72 students with a comparatively low degree of imagibility, resulting from its minimal role in credentialing and from the amorphous nature of the Associate's degree. For some students, particularly those whose Associate degree "majors" can be described only as "General Studies" or "Liberal Arts and Sciences," the Associate's degree was but an advanced high school diploma, serving as a warrantee, so to speak, of general learning. There is nothing wrong with that. In fact, given the well-documented decline of the quality of learning in U.S. secondary schools, such programs are necessary, and the community college is one of their principal providers.

The Proximate Institution

The second major theme concerns the populations served by the community college. Given its occasional roles, minimal costs, and ease of access, the community college, by its very nature, can reach a broader spectrum of American society than other types of postsecondary institutions. This reach is augmented by the sheer number and geographical distribution of community colleges.

While recent (1986) data show that the proportion of minority students who are U. S. citizens is higher in community colleges (22.5%) than among undergraduates in 4-year institutions (16.6%),[15] for reasons of proximity to one's primary residence, the community college inevitably will serve the majority more than minorities. Outside the South and parts of the Southwest, for example, rural America is heavily white, and the principal postsecondary presence in rural areas is either the community college or the state college. As Grubb (1988) pointed out, the highest enrollment rate in community colleges in the country is in the state of Washington (22.9% of the eligible population), a state in which over 90% of the population is white, and in which there are 20 community colleges outside Seattle, Tacoma and Spokane.

With a little more work, I believe the NLS–72 data can demonstrate an old rule of elasticity of supply: when the only provider is X, X provides to (a) the dominant ethnic population, and (b) to students of all ages. So if the community college, considered nationally, serves an older population (as well as a younger one), it is the result of elementary economics. For the same reasons, the community college winds up serving a higher proportion of white, Hispanic, and Native American students than black students (who will make extra efforts to attend a Historically Black College). We also know that rural populations are more likely to be classified in the low and medium SES ranges than metropolitan populations. So for those who select postsecondary institutions on the basis of proximity, as many students do (A. Astin, Green, and Korn, 1987), community colleges will inevitably be the principal providers, hence will wind up serving a higher proportion of low and moderate SES students than will other types of educational institutions.

In this respect, the community college is not like our religious or cultural institutions. Its "liturgy" (curriculum) is non-sectarian, and there's no need for more than one in town (or county, or city district). From another perspective, while there are variations in that liturgy, they do not depend on visiting exhibits or performers: they are resident.

Indeed, the curricular liturgy of the community college is fairly consistent. We can infer what the community college offers from what students take; what it seems to offer is a combination of specialized curricula in three major occupational fields (allied health, business and business support services, and engineering technologies), and general studies curricula dominated by the social sciences. Students interested principally in either the sciences or the humanities either do not attend community colleges at all or transfer very quickly. Common sense would conclude that there is no way these institutions could offer enough depth in the basic sciences or the humanities to reach the "trapgates" of the fields. The transcripts confirm such a hypothesis.

Within this theme, the transcripts also suggest significant sex stereotyping in curricula pursued, hinting that students were advised into traditional roles (Kirby, 1981; Gittel, 1986). Women who pursued community college occupational education in the mid- and late 1970s did so principally in office support services, allied health, nursing, retail marketing, education, and applied arts. These fields accounted for nearly 70% of the occupational Associate's degrees awarded to women in the NLS/PETS. On the other hand, two-thirds of the men who earned occupational Associate's degrees did so in agriculture, business administration, computer-related fields, engineering technologies, protective services, and precision production/repair.[16] This theme is somewhat troubling, particularly in light of the spectacular rise in the overall educational attainment of women over the past two decades.

IV. Defenders and Critics: Reflections on an Old Debate

Having read a good deal of the record, and having reflected briefly on the nature of the community college as both an occasional and proximate institution, let's go back to the debate between the functionalist defenders of the community college and what Dougherty (1987) calls the "class reproduction school" of community college critics. To put it too simply, the "functionalists" say that the community college is the best vehicle for equal opportunity in postsecondary education; their opponents counter that the community college does nothing but perpetuate existing inequalities in American society. Both schools may now take what they wish from the transcripts; but I think the entire NLS-72 database ultimately helps us transcend this unproductive debate.

Hocus-Pocus Research

Three points need to be raised about the research used in the work of both defenders and detractors.

First, I am baffled by the construction of variables and estimates in most of the work bearing on this debate. Without the transcripts, for example, it is nearly impossible to determine precisely who is on a transfer/academic track in a community college and who isn't. What the student responds on a survey form or what he or she tells the registrar is not necessarily what he or she actually does.[17] Without the transcripts, it is nearly impossible to determine who changed from one track to another—and when. Having read, line-by-line, the complete academic records of over 10,000 students in the NLS/PETS, I am not sure that the construct of "track" itself is very helpful. On so many occasions, the community college portions of student records showed individuals starting out with a combination of basic skills courses and introductions to the disciplines and professions, then selecting more and more courses in a given field, as if they were choosing a "major" (and regardless of whether they actually received a degree).[18] This pattern is almost identical to that of students working through the curricula of 4-year institutions (except that, in 4-year institutions there is less work in basic skills and more in introductory college-level skills, for example, students take College Algebra or Finite Math instead of Pre-Collegiate Algebra). From the general to the focused. Should we be upset that community college students do it just like 4-year college students do it? Is this phenomenon properly called "tracking"?

Second, the literature on both sides evidences considerable confusion and outright naivete concerning aspirations and plans with respect to the "baccalaureate degree." Using a metaphor from the nightly newscasts, the Bachelor's degree is the Dow Jones Industrial

Average of U.S. higher education. That is, everybody has heard of it. When people ask "What did the Market do today?" they mean the Dow Jones, and that's the answer they get, even though it is not the real answer to their question. What we have done in the semantic shorthand of our culture is to equate "Dow Jones" and "Market." We have done the same with "Bachelor's Degree" and "College Degree," let alone "Higher Education Attainment." In fact, in the language and rhetoric of the critics' discourse, "a degree" is shorthand for the Bachelor's.

The Associate's degree, on the other hand, is like the NASDAQ average of Over-the-Counter stocks: virtually nobody knows what it is or how to interpret it. In contrast, the Bachelor's degree is a culturally visible symbol with significant power in public policy. No congressional committee, for example, asks the U.S. Department of Education for trends in production of Associate's degrees. They don't ask for the NASDAQ average: they want the Dow Jones. And what is true for congressional committees is even more true for 18-year-old high school seniors, let alone their parents.

So when we look at "aspirations" we are looking at attachments to culturally visible and powerful symbols, even if those symbols are vaguely understood. Those of us who have administered the Cooperative Institutional Research Program (CIRP) survey to entering college freshmen know that a significant proportion do not understand what various degrees either mean or require.[19] Furthermore, the intensity of one's "aspirations" ranges widely, from casual to committed (Alexander and Cook, 1979). When we look at "plans," on the other hand, we get closer to the individual's sense of his or her realistic options, and these seem to rely less on the most visible and powerful symbol of postsecondary educational attainment in our society. Inheriting their constructs from Clark's (1960a) "cooling out" thesis, none of the defenders or critics bother with this distinction, even though the NLS-72 provides the opportunity to explore it.

Third, when it deals with the economic outcomes of education, the literature is often bizarre. The most notable and persistent of the critics (Karabel, 1972; Karabel, 1986; Pincus, 1980; Pincus and Archer, 1989; Brint and Karabel, 1989) perform hocus-pocus analyses of secondary sources. They take other scholars' studies, state system studies, institutional studies, and census data—all with different samples, different populations, different years (boom or bust), different definitions of variables—utter an incantation, and pretend that it all makes sense. When it doesn't make sense, they challenge their opponents, the defenders of community colleges, to prove that it does make sense. The defenders, in turn, are even more helpless because, as the critics correctly point out, they are trapped by the propaganda machines of organizations that seek increased funding (federal, state, local) for community colleges. When there is money on the table, no one will admit to either flaws or ambiguity in institutional performance. No one wants to look directly at unobtrusively obtained national data.

Measuring Mobility

Lastly, the debate relies heavily on the effects of community colleges, principally in terms of social mobility. But the debate takes place in a comparative vacuum of meaningful effects. That is, with the exception of Monk-Turner's work (1983) based on the National Longitudinal Surveys of Labor Market Experience (another set of archives housed at Ohio State University), none of the studies of this issue analyzed by Dougherty (1987) have truly long-term employment, occupation, or earnings data, let alone information on family formation, home ownership, or anything else that would allow comparison of the SES of children to that of their parents. With the fifth (1986) followup, the NLS-72 archive now provides such data, at least through age 32/33.[20] Let's look at some of the variables that would be used in constructing SES ratings for the NLS-72 students at "thirtysomething."

Occupational Plans v. Occupational Realities

There are two ways of considering the occupational distribution of community college attendees at age 32/33. The first, presented in Table 22, selects 31 specific jobs within 5 broad occupational areas (business, technical, health services, production/operations, and human services). The presentation allows us to see the distribution of groups with specific educational histories across those occupations.

Among business occupations, for example, the distinction between accountants and bookkeepers is notable: the former draws a high percentage of those with Bachelor's degrees and 4-year college backgrounds, the latter draws a moderate percentage of those who either never attended college or never earned a degree of any kind. Terminal Associate's degree holders tend to turn up in managerial/administrative jobs in manufacturing industries in roughly the same proportion as do former 4-year college students, but that distribution does not hold for managerial/administrative jobs in financial service industries.

While I cannot explain why a comparatively high percentage of transfer students who earned Bachelor's degrees wind up as personnel workers, the direct relationship between terminal occupational Associate's degrees and ultimate occupation stands out clearly in the cases of electronic technicians, health technicians, and nurses.

There are hosts of fascinating relationships displayed in Table 22 that deserve further investigation. My point in laying out a complex picture of occupational distribution in relation to educational background is to indicate that the routes we take from schooling to work are not always linear. In fact, contrary to the claims of both defenders (e.g., Roueche and Baker, 1987) and critics (e.g., Pincus, 1980; Pincus, 1986), attending a 4-year college does not straighten the line between education and work any more than does attending a community college.

A second way of looking at the occupational distribution of students in the NLS-72 cohort at age 32 is with reference to their plans at age 19. This portrait, set forth in Table 23, brings us flush against the contention of community college critics from Clark (1960a) to

Brint and Karabel (1989) that community colleges—far more than 4-year colleges—frustrate the ambitions of students who attend. The early critics such as Clark never had the large scale, long-term data of NLS-72, particularly with its transcripts as a sorting mechanism. The later critics seemed to ignore such data or used it without the transcripts. In neither earlier nor later analyses were the kind of data set forth in Table 23 considered.

Table 23 compares occupational expectations at age 19 with occupational realities at age 32 for five groups. The first group consists of community college students who earned more than 10 credits from community colleges but no degree higher than the Associate's. This group, in turn, is split between those who earned no degree whatsoever by the time they were 30, and those who earned either a certificate or Associate's degree. Second, we take 4-year college students who never attended a community college and who earned more than 10 credits from one or more 4-year colleges. They, too, are divided in two groups: those who earned no degree whatsoever by the time they were 30, and those who earned at least a Bachelor's degree. Lastly, we have those students who, to the best of our knowledge, did not attend any kind of postsecondary institution by the time they were 30.

What do we see? First, as a rule, the hopes of youth exceed the realities of age. That's the way we are. No matter where people go to school or what degree they earn (if any), they wind up at age 32 doing something other than what they had planned at 19, and what they wind up doing tends to have less "status." Does this surprise anyone? As teenagers, we dream of becoming Nobel prize winners—or the equivalent; by "thirtysome-thing" we forget Nobel's first name (assuming we ever knew it) or how he blasted his way into history, and are happy to have steady jobs, to be respected in our work, able to pay the rent, take a vacation, and raise our children well. Is this, as the critics imply, a national tragedy?

In fact, when asked if they were satisfied with the progress of their careers at age 26 (unfortunately, this question was not asked at age 32), 82.5% of those employed said yes. Among those who had "made a go" at postsecondary education, the only feature of personal history that distinguished the most satisfied from the least satisfied was an earned degree of any kind, including a terminal Associate's degree from a community college.

Indeed (and secondly), people who do not earn degrees are more likely to wind up in "lower status" occupations than they originally planned than are those who did earn degrees. Does that surprise anyone? What may surprise some is that this phenomenon applies equally to community college students, 4-year college students, and students who never went to college. For example, a higher percentage of NLS-72 community college students who earned terminal Associate's degrees wound up in "professional" occupations (26.5%) than 4-year college students who did not earn a Bachelor's degree (20.9%).

Third, the background "noise" of occupational life is commerce, an area that, to the typical 19-year old, is vast and unknown. We are more likely to fade into this background by the time we are in our early 30s—as managers, administrators, salespersons, and buyers—

than we ever imagined, and less likely to invest the considerable time, effort, and energy in additional schooling to become professional workers.

The literature that criticizes community colleges for thwarting the aspirations of their students often uses the occupational category of "manager" as a privileged class. Given the number of people who call themselves "managers" in any survey, the occupation hardly represents an elite. As an occupational category, "manager" covers vast territories, from CEOs to the proprietor of the local dry cleaning establishment to the administrator of the county recreation department's evening programs. It sounds somewhat strained to call the people who inhabit this territory a privileged class. In general, as Table 23 shows, a higher percentage of people wind up in this category than originally aspired to it, whether they went to a 2-year college, a 4-year college or no college (the only exception involves terminal Associate's degree holders).

The category, "professional," is also misused in the critical literature. If, at age 19, I say I want to be an actor, am I aspiring to a "profession" in the same sense as "lawyer" or "dentist" or "college professor"? And, given the wages of dinner theaters and regional theaters, is acting an "elite" occupation?

The literature critical of community colleges for thwarting the aspirations of students to become "professionals" never tells us what it means by "professional," nor justifies the putative "professions" as elite or privileged classes. Are schoolteachers members of a profession? You bet! Are they a privileged or elite class? Tell that to the 2.5 million schoolteachers in this country! As Table 23 demonstrates by using three explicit categories of "professionals" (including schoolteachers), <u>even if</u> one defines "professions" in terms of those generally requiring a <u>post</u>-baccalaureate degree (the NLS-72 category I label "Professional II"), community college attendance has no greater negative impact on occupational aspirations than 4-year college attendance. In fact, in both types of institutions, the more significant determinant of whether one's aspirations to become a "professional" were fulfilled was whether or not one earned a degree. This phenomenon should also surprise no one: what makes professions "professions," in part, is that they require certified, specialized knowledge, and the certification is reflected in the degree.

Earnings

As a component of SES, earnings is a critical variable, and Table 24 presents the earnings of NLS-72 students in their most recent full-time jobs in 1985, by community college attendance pattern. Looking at the 1985 data, there is no clear-cut pattern that would lead us to conclude that community college attendance is a drag on earnings—at least through age 32/33. The highest paid group attended community college, and the lowest paid group did not. This pattern held for men, and women with children (by age 32/33). The greatest differentials between the earnings of men and both groups of women (those with children, and those without children), however, occurred in categories of community college attendance in which no degree was earned. For women who attended community colleges, then, earning a degree had a greater impact on earnings at thirtysomething than was the case for men.

We also note (and Table 26 reveals a similar pattern) that terminal Associate's degree holders earned less than those who were non-incidental attendees but never earned any degree. This is not a new observation (see, e.g., Pincus, 1980; Nunley and Breneman, 1988). Why does this happen? It happens, in part, because the non-graduate has more years of job experience. But it happens more because a higher percentage of the non-graduates wind up in business-related occupations that, at age 32, pay better than occupations in health care fields dominated by terminal Associate's degree holders. And it happens even more because women are a majority of terminal Associate's degree holders, and women are unquestionably the victims of inequities in the labor market that have nothing to do with educational attainment (Adelman, 1991).

Home Ownership

Another potential component of SES is home ownership. In this case, we can examine home ownership rates at age 32 by socioeconomic status at age 18, using college attendance patterns as an intermediate variable. Table 25 does so. If we focus on students who were in the lowest SES quartile at age 18, hence least likely to come from families that owned their homes, we see that the highest rates of home ownership at age 32 were among those who attended community colleges and whose highest degree was the Associate's. The lowest rates of home ownership among this group were for people who attended community colleges, transferred to 4-year colleges, and subsequently earned a Bachelor's degree. Once again, there is no clear-cut pattern. One cannot conclude that community college attendance either hinders or advances the chances of home ownership. The relationship between home ownership and college attendance pattern is, in fact, rather tenuous.

General Economic Mobility

But in terms of economic mobility, the critics have a point that is strongly borne out by the NLS-72 data. Table 26 looks at 1985 earnings, unemployment, and job experience by both postsecondary attendance pattern and SES in 1972. Basically the table answers the question, "What patterns of postsecondary attendance are most likely to minimize unemployment, maximize earnings, and move an individual from a lower to a higher SES category?"

What do we see in Table 26? As Jencks *et al* (1972) observed, SES has a lasting impact on economic status. It takes a lot of work to override one's initial circumstances, whether one starts out in the lowest or the highest brackets. If we focus only on those students who did not continue their education after high school, we see exactly the same economic positions 14 years later. Even with no postsecondary education, as initial SES rises, wages rise, mean years of job experience rise, and unemployment drops. The only postsecondary attendance pattern that consistently overcomes initial economic circumstance is that of 4-year college attendance, whether or not a Bachelor's degree was earned.

This is an unfortunate aspect of the way we are. It is unfortunate in terms of the community college role because so many community college attendees in the NLS–72 sample seemed to use the institution for genuine purposes of learning, irrespective of social outcomes. Their behavior says that intentional learning is ingrained in us, whether that learning is incidental or continuous, whether it is basic general education or occupationally oriented, whether it is undertaken for enlightenment or the acquisition of specific skills. It is an article of our faith that learning ought to be rewarded, and that is one of the major normative messages of educational institutions.

There may be a brighter side to this matter that the account given in these pages does not reach. The most significant work to date on these data (Conaty, Alsalam, James, and To, 1989) uses the transcripts to demonstrate that, with few exceptions, <u>what one studies</u> has a greater impact on earnings at age 32 than where one attended college. To be sure, the subjects of the Conaty, *et al* study were the Bachelor's degree recipients; but if the relationships between coursetaking and earnings (controlling for college major, SAT scores, SES, etc.) are significant, then we ought to examine those relationships among community college attendees before we conclude that the normative message of community colleges remains unfulfilled.

V. Is Life So Cold? Concluding Thoughts About the Way We Are

Roughly one-quarter of the NLS–72 generation attended community colleges in different ways, and they represent a more typical segment of the population of high school graduates (race, sex, socioeconomic status) then either those who attended only 4-year colleges, those who attended only proprietary or vocational schools, or those who never continued their education at all. They clustered around the averages of just about everything. What does their behavior tell us about the way we are?

First, that we use major normative institutions for utilitarian purposes, and that our relationships with those institutions are more occasional and *ad hoc* than otherwise. We recognize the value of education, but once schooling ceases to be compulsory, we tend to go to school only on our own terms.

Second, that we are more interested in learning, in acquiring new skills, and in completing our basic general education than in advanced credentials, even if those credentials yield greater economic rewards. At the same time, to the extent to which we acquired strong academic backgrounds in the course of our compulsory schooling, we are more likely to complete postcompulsory schooling of any kind, academic or occupational.

Third, while we are genuinely committed to lifelong learning, we nonetheless concentrate formal learning at early stages of our lives. We are children of time and its conventions. We do not easily break from cultural traditions of when to do what. Perhaps we know that the more distant we are from formal education, the more difficult it is to recapture both knowledge and the discipline of schooling.

Fourth, our general knowledge is just that—general and introductory. The time we typically allow for schooling does not permit depth. So we grasp for something particular, something we perceive as related to current or future work. The result is that we may know more about what we do for a living, but are less adaptable to changes in the conditions or opportunities of work. If there is a just complaint about what community colleges allow us to do, it lies here (Pincus, 1986).

Lastly, our youthful aspirations and hopes exceed what actually happens to us, no matter what we do in between. Does that mean we should abandon them? If life itself is a "cooling-out" process, does that mean we should spend most of it moping about what could have been or blaming "the system" for what didn't happen to us? Do we adopt the position that only the 1% of the population at "the command posts of the American occupational structure" (Karabel and Astin, 1975), only the movie stars, succeed in our society and that everyone else fails? everyone else is a victim? everyone else doesn't count?

Aspirations and hopes usually translate into effort, and effort makes something better than what otherwise would have been—for individuals, groups, and the nation. And while we all gripe about our lives and fortunes, if that's all we do, we freeze ourselves out of efforts to improve the lives and fortunes of our children. The Class of '72 did not throw in the towel. We can't afford to, either.

Notes

1. The "public release" data tapes for the NLS–72 transcripts contain considerable inaccuracies, and the process of cleaning them—with sponsorship of the National Science Foundation, the U.S. Department of Labor, and the Office of Research of the U.S. Department of Education—took over 2 years. For an account of both the dirt and the cleaning process, see the "Introduction" to *A College Course Map* (Adelman, 1990a). Over 20% of the degrees in the original database were misclassified (e.g., Associate's degrees that should have been Bachelor's, and vice versa) or missing, and, while I did not compute precise percentages for them, problems of similar magnitude existed with respect to dates of degrees, dates of attendance, and majors. Unfortunately, the few researchers who have used the NLS-72 transcripts have produced data that are simply not credible in light of the cleaning. For a telling example, Grubb (1991, p. 200) says that 43.8% of the students who attended 4-year colleges earned a Bachelor's degree within "7 years" of high school graduation. While I am not sure how Grubb measures "7 years," the cleaned transcripts show 61.7% of those who entered 4-year colleges earning Bachelor's degrees by December 31, 1979, roughly 7.5 years from the average high school graduation date. The cleaned transcript files are scheduled to be released by the National Center for Education Statistics on CD-ROM, with an accompanying electronic codebook, in 1992.

2. When one uses transcripts, the keys to a census of community college students depend, in large part, on how one defines a community college, a "public technical institute," and a "private vocational school." In the cleaned version of the NLS-72 transcripts, the status of each college or school was reviewed in light of the 1975 Carnegie typology and the nature of credentials actually awarded to NLS-72 students. I invented a new "Carnegie" code for what Grubb (1991) calls "public technical institutes" (generally, Area Vocational Technical Institutes), and distinguished them from public 2-year technical colleges (which remained in the universe of "community colleges)." And with few exceptions (each handled on a case-by-case basis), no institution that actually awarded degrees higher than the Associate's to students in the NLS/PETS was classified as a community college.

3. This monograph is one of a series under the working title, "Archives of a Generation," which includes *Light and Shadows on College Athletes* (Adelman, 1990b) and *Women at Thirtysomething: Paradoxes of Attainment* (Adelman, 1991).

4. Given problems with missing term dates on some transcripts, and the tendency of some people to enroll simultaneously in both community colleges and 4-year institutions, it was not always possible to use first and last dates of attendance in the logic that generated the attendance-pattern taxonomy.

5. All percentage figures used in this and the other related studies of NLS-72 are "weighted." This means that each person in the initial (1972) sample represented X number of people with the same characteristics in the general population of high school graduates, and a formula weights them so that they can perform that representative function in the database. As we proceeded through the years of the NLS-72 surveys and transcript sample, this initial weight was modified according to an individual's participation in these subsequent "panels." Depending on the question being asked and the population under consideration, I use either one or three different weights from a collection of eight different weights.

6. For those NLS-72 students who attended 4-year colleges only, the weighted percentages in each of the six attendance patterns, 1972-1984, were:

Earned BA, attended only one 4-year college:	36.9%
Earned BA, attended more than one college:	24.2
No BA, and earned >59 credits:	12.4
No BA, and earned 11-59 credits:	18.3
Incidental 4-year, earning <11 credits:	5.2
Other 4-year pattern:	2.9

7. "To the best of our knowledge." Some may have enrolled, but we were unable to obtain confirming transcripts for them. Other evidence in the survey data suggests that 12% of this group (slightly more than 5% of the entire NLS-72 sample) did enroll.

8. Fetters, Stowe, and Owings (1984) demonstrated that students over-report (or parents under-report) the dominance of a second language in their households, but that the agreement between students and parents on this issue is higher in the case of Spanish than it is, for example, in Italian, Chinese, or German.

9. Opening fall enrollment data reported to the U.S. Department of Education indicate the following percentages in the ethnic distribution of community college students, 1976–1988:

Race/Ethnicity	1976	1980	1984	1988
White	80.2%	79.8%	78.5%	77.0%
Black	11.2	10.6	10.3	9.8
Hispanic	5.5	5.7	6.5	8.0
Asian-American	2.1	2.8	3.7	4.1
Native American	1.1	1.1	1.0	1.0

From Snyder, T.D., *Digest of Education Statistics, 1990,* Table 190, p. 199.

10. There are a number of ways to identify those who served in the military among the members of the NLS-72. One way is to use a special file created in 1986 that merged the records of the NLS-72 with the comprehensive data of the Defense Manpower Data Center (DMDC)—at least through 1979. Since DMDC keeps records on everyone who ever either applied to, enlisted, or otherwise served in the U.S. Military, this procedure sounds like an unassailable unobtrusive way of identifying these people. The merged NLS/DMDC data file, however, does not include women, and, up to 1976, confuses applicants and actual "accessions" (Kolstad, 1987). A second method is to use the NLS-72 surveys, which asked questions about military service through 1979. Unfortunately, the 1986 survey asked about military service only for those who were on active duty during the first week of February, 1986. The data file thus misses anyone who may have entered and left the military between October of 1979 and February of 1986. For purposes of relating military service to college attendance, the survey responses through 1979 are adequate, but not perfect.

11. Only 9,000 students of the 22,600 in the sample answered these questions in the Base Year (1972) Survey. Had I relied on those responses only, minority students would have been under-represented. The "1973 First Followup/Supplementary Survey" picked up most of the others. But the response categories were slightly different. I normalized the response categories for the aspirations/plans variables. The classification logic basically said, "If the student did not answer the question in 1972, give us his or her answer in 1973 in the combined 1972/1973 taxonomy of responses." The result yielded codable responses for 21,300 students, with adequate minority representation.

12. The Base Year (1972) respondents were asked to project their most likely activity during the following year (1973). The response categories included taking vocational/trade/ business courses at a trade school, taking vocational/trade/business courses at a community college, and taking academic courses at community colleges. Matched against their long-term educational plans, here is how they responded:

Long-Term Educational Plans
(All rows add to 100.0%)

Likely activity in 1973	H.S. only	Voc./bus.	CC/Assc.	4-yr./BA	Graduate school
Vocation/business in vocational school	3.7%	81.7%	8.1%	4.1%	2.4%
Vocation/business in community college	2.3	19.7	52.9	20.4	4.7
Academic courses in community college	1.5	5.6	41.0	38.6	13.3
4-year college	0.7	1.6	1.9	69.5	26.3

13. At various points in the NLS-72 surveys, respondents who did not continue their education were asked why they did not continue. Of those who never entered any kind of postsecondary institution by age 30, 24.7% had said (when they were 19) that they didn't continue at that time because they "didn't like or need school."

14. Looking at all NLS-72 students who earned Associate's degrees from community colleges, and comparing the terminal A.A. holders with those who also earned B.A.s, we note substantial differences in community college program:

Associate degree program	Terminal Associate's from community college	Associate's from community college and Bachelor's
Arts and Sciences	16.9%	44.1%
General Studies	12.8	25.1
Business/Accounting	10.3	9.8
Technical/Computer	10.8	4.0
Health/Nursing	17.4	4.5
Other Vocational	31.8	12.5

In examining the transcripts of these students, the "General Studies" designation was applied to those programs in which more than a third of the credits were earned outside the traditional arts and sciences disciplines.

15. Using Tables 175 and 176 from the *Digest of Education Statistics, 1989* (Snyder, 1989), here are the calculations for the proportion of undergraduate, minority students in both 2-year and 4-year colleges in 1986 (U.S. citizens only). These are enrollment figures, in millions:

	2-year	4-year	Total
A.Total Enrollment	4,671	7,818	12,489
(minus Graduate Students	—	1,432	1,432)
(minus 1st Professional	—	270	270)
(minus non-resident aliens who are undergraduates	53	151	204)
A1. Net Domestic Undergrads	**4,618**	**5,965**	**10,583**
B.Total Domestic Minority	1,040	1,194	2,234
(minus Graduate Students	—	166	166)
(minus 1st Professional	—	136	136)
B1. Net Domestic Minority	**1,040**	**992**	**2,032**
C. A1 divided by B1	**22.5%**	**16.6%**	**19.2%**

16. One can infer from national survey data that this sex stereotyping was considerably modulated by the mid-1980s. In 1984-5, for example, women earned just about half of the community college Associate's degrees in computer-related fields, while men earned 58.7% of the degrees in fine and applied arts. Black women also earned 40% of the degrees in protective services, a marked departure from gender ratios among other racial groups. (Snyder, 1989, p. 224).

17. I have never understood how researchers could classify community college students as pursuing an occupational or general program without actually examining the student records. What a students says on a survey form that he or she is doing is not necessarily what he or she does. Here, for example, are the courses taken by an Associate's degree recipient who listed "engineering technology" as the "major":

Microbiology	Marriage and Family
Games and Exercises	Psychology of Adjustment
Calculus I	Principles of Economics
History of the U.S.	Social Problems
Texas Government	Architectural Drawing
Engineering Drawing	Organic Chemistry
Principles of Accounting	Introductory Sociology
Introduction to Business	Business Communications
Calculus II	Basic Technical Drawing

This is not the record of someone with an occupational major, certainly not one in "engineering technology," though there is no question that the individual has developed an employable skill through three courses in technical drawing.

18. Using the dirty public release data tapes for the NLS-/PETS, Grubb (1991) classified "academic" or "vocational" community college students on the basis of what they did in their first semester, as follows: "academic students are defined as those with more than half their credits in academic subjects during their first semester, excluding those entering for obviously vocational reasons" (p. 204). Under this definition, a student who takes a course entitled, "Mathematics: Foundations" for 3 credits, "Body-Building" for 1 credit, and "College Orientation" for 1 credit is deemed an "academic student." This is, *prima facie*, absurd, and is even more absurd because the course taxonomy in the public release data tapes cannot tell Grubb whether "Mathematics: Foundations" is a remedial course or a college-level course.

19. In 4 years of administering the CIRP to freshmen in a large state college, I found that 20% of them could not provide intelligible answers to the two sequential restricted response questions: "What is the highest degree you intend to attain?" and "What is the highest degree you intend to get from this institution?" That is, in 20% of the cases, the answer to the second question was "higher" than the answer to the first, i.e., students were checking off degrees concerning which they were largely ignorant.

20. Some 74% of the NLS-72 participants in the 5th (1986) Follow-Up Survey were 32 years old at the time; another 23% were 33 or older; and 3% were 31. For purposes of convenience, I sometimes refer to them collectively as "32/33" years old.

References

Adelman, C. 1990a. *A College Course Map: Taxonomy and Transcript Data.* Washington, D.C.: U.S. Government Printing Office.

Adelman, C. 1990b. *Light and Shadows on College Athletes.* Washington, D.C.: U.S. Government Printing Office.

Adelman, C. 1991. *Women at Thirtysomething: Paradoxes of Attainment.* Washington, D.C.: U.S. Government Printing Office.

Alba, R. D. and Lavin, D.E. 1981. "Community Colleges and Tracking in Higher Education." *Sociology of Education* 54: 223-237.

Alexander, K. L. and Cook, M. 1979. "The Motivational Relevance of Educational Plans: Questioning the Conventional Wisdom." *Social Psychology Quarterly* 42: 202-213.

Alexander, K. L., Holupka, S. and Pallas, A.M. 1987. "Social Background and Academic Determinants of Two-Year versus Four-Year College Attendance: Evidence from Two Cohorts a Decade Apart." *American Journal of Education*, 96: 57-80.

Alsalam, N. and Rogers, G. T. 1991. *The Condition of Education, 1991.* Volume 2. Washington, D.C.: National Center for Education Statistics.

Anderson, K. L. 1981. "Post-High School Experiences and College Attrition." *Sociology of Education* 54: 1–15.

Astin, A. W. 1982. *Minorities in American Higher Education.* San Francisco: Jossey-Bass.

Astin, A. W. 1984. "Student Involvement: a Developmental Theory for Higher Education." *Journal of College Student Personnel* 25: 277–308.

Astin, A.W., Green, K. C. and Korn, W. S. 1987. *The American Freshman: Twenty Year Trends.* Los Angeles: Higher Education Research Institute.

Breneman, D. W. and Nelson, S. C. 1981. *Financing Community Colleges: an Economic Perspective.* Washington, D.C.: the Brookings Institution.

Brint, S. and Karabel, J. 1989. *The Diverted Dream: Community Colleges and the Promise of Educational Opportunity in America, 1900–1985.* New York: Oxford University Press.

Clark, B. 1960a. "The 'Cooling-out' Function in Higher Education." *American Journal of Sociology* 65: 560–576.

Clark, B. 1960b. *The Open-Door College.* New York: McGraw-Hill.

Cohen, A. M. 1988. "Degree Achievement by Minorities in Community Colleges." *Review of Higher Education* 11: 383–402.

Cohen, A. M. and Brawer, F. B. 1982. *The American Community College.* San Francisco: Jossey-Bass.

Cohen, A. M. and Brawer, F. B. 1987. *The Collegiate Function of Community Colleges.* San Francisco: Jossey-Bass.

Conaty, J., Alsalam, N., James, E. and To, D-L. 1989. "College Quality and Future Earnings: Where Should You Send Your Sons and Daughters to College?" Paper presented at the annual meeting of the American Sociological Association.

deArmas, C.P. and McDavis, R.J. 1981. "White, Black, and Hispanic Students' Perceptions of a Community College Environment." *Journal of College Student Personnel* 22: 337–41.

Dougherty, K. 1987. "The Effects of Community Colleges: Aid or Hindrance to Socio-economic Attainment?" *Sociology of Education* 60: 86–103.

Educational Testing Service. 1991. *Performance at the Top: from Elementary Through Graduate School.* Princeton, N.J.: Author.

Fetters, W. B., Stowe, P.S., and Owings, J. A. 1984. *Quality of Responses of High School Students to Questionnaire Items.* Washington, D.C.: National Center for Education Statistics.

Folger, J. K., Astin, H. S., and Bayer, A. E. 1970. *Human Resources and Higher Education.* New York: Russell Sage.

Gittell, M. 1986. "A Place for Women?" In Zwerling, L. S. (ed.), *The Community College and Its Critics.* San Francisco: Jossey-Bass, 71–80.

Grubb, W. N. 1988. "Vocationalizing Higher Education: the Causes of Enrollment and Completion in Two-Year Colleges, 1970–1980." *Economics of Education Review* 7: 301–19.

Grubb, W. N. 1989. "The Effects of Differentiation on Educational Attainment: the Case of Community Colleges." *Review of Higher Education* 12: 349–374.

Grubb, W. N. 1991. "The Decline of Community College Transfer Rates." *Journal of Higher Education* 62: 194–217.

Hilton, T. L. and Lee, V. E. 1988. "Student Interest and Persistence in Science." *Journal of Higher Education* 59: 510–526.

Jencks, C. et al. 1972. *Inequality: a Reassessment of the Effect of Family and Schooling in America.* New York: Basic Books.

Karabel, J. 1972. "Community Colleges and Social Stratification." *Harvard Educational Review* 42: 521-61.

Karabel, J. 1986. "Community Colleges and Social Stratification in the 1980s." In Zwerling, L. S. (ed.), *The Community College and Its Critics.* San Francisco: Jossey-Bass, 13-30.

Karabel, J. and Astin, A. W. 1975. "Social Class, Academic Ability, and College 'Quality'." *Social Forces* 53: 381-398.

Kirby, E.B. 1981. "Petticoats to Jackhammers: Strategies for Women in Occupational Education." In Eaton, J. S. (ed.), *Women in Community Colleges.* San Francisco: Jossey-Bass, pp. 43-53.

Knepper, P. 1989. *Student Progress in College: NLS-72 Postsecondary Education Transcript Study.* Washington, D.C.: National Center for Education Statistics (CS#89-411).

Kolstad, A. 1987. *NLS-72/DMDC Military Records: Data File User's Manual.* Washington, D.C.: National Center for Education Statistics, (CS#87-383).

Levin B. and Clowes, D. 1980. "Realization of Educational Aspirations Among Blacks and Whites in Two- and Four-Year Colleges." *Community/Junior College Research Quarterly* 4: 185-193.

London, H. B. 1978. *The Culture of a Community College.* New York: Praeger.

Monk-Turner, E. 1983. "Sex, Educational Differentiation, and Occupational Status." *Sociological Quarterly* 24: 393-404.

Neumann, W. and Riesman, D. 1980. "The Community College Elite." In Vaughan, G. B. (ed.) *Questioning the Community College Role.* San Francisco: Jossey-Bass, pp. 53-72.

Nunley, C. R. and Breneman, D. W. 1988. "Defining and Measuring Quality in Community College Education." In Eaton, J. S. (ed.), *Colleges of Choice.* New York: ACE/Macmillan, 62-92.

Pascarella, E. T. et al. 1986. "Long-Term Persistence of Two-Year College Students." Paper presented at the annual convention of the Association for the Study of Higher Education. ED #268-900.

Pincus, F.L. 1980. "The False Promises of Community Colleges: Class Conflict and Vocational Education." *Harvard Educational Review* 60: 332-61.

Pincus, F. L. 1986. "Vocational Education: More False Promises." In Zwerling, S. L. (ed.), *The Community College and Its Critics*. San Francisco: Jossey-Bass, 41-52.

Pincus, F.L. and Archer, E. 1989. *Bridges to Opportunity: are Community Colleges Meeting the Transfer Needs of Minority Students?* New York: Academy for Educational Development.

Richardson, R. C. Jr. 1988. "The Presence of Access and the Pursuit of Achievement." In Eaton, J. S. (ed.), *Colleges of Choice*. New York: ACE/McMillan, 25-46.

Roueche, J. and Baker, G. 1987. *Access and Excellence: the Open Door Colleges*. Washington, D.C.: Community College Press.

Snyder, T. D. 1989. *Digest of Education Statistics, 1989*. Washington, D.C.: National Center for Education Statistics.

Stage, F. 1988. "Student Typologies and the Study of College Outcomes." *The Review of Higher Education* 11: 247-258.

Tinto, V. 1987. *Leaving College: Rethinking the Causes and Cures of Student Attrition*. Chicago: Univ. of Chicago Press.

Tourangeau, R. et al. 1987. *The National Longitudinal Study of the High School Class of 1972: Fifth (1986) Follow-Up Data User's Manual*. Washington, DC: National Center for Education Statistics.

Velez, W. 1985. "Finishing College: the Effects of College Type." *Sociology of Education* 58: 191-200.

Velez, W. and Javalgi, R. G. 1987. "Two-Year College to Four-Year College: the Likelihood of Transfer." *American Journal of Education* 96: 81-94.

Zwerling, L. S. 1976. *Second Best: the Crisis of the Community College*. New York: McGraw-Hill.

Zwerling, L. S. 1986. "Lifelong Learning: a New Form of Tracking." In Zwerling, L. S. (ed.), *The Community College and Its Critics*. San Francisco: Jossey-Bass, 53-60.

Table 1.—Basic community college attendance pattern, by race and sex

Attendance pattern	All	Race/ethnicity			Sex	
		White	Black	Hispanic	Male	Female
Transfer: AA + BA	3.4% (.067)	3.6% (.075)	1.1% (.100)	2.9% (.171)	3.8% (.104)	2.9% (.080)
Transfer: BA/no AA	3.3 (.071)	3.4 (.071)	2.7 (.176)	2.1 (.447)	3.7 (.113)	2.8 (.069)
Transfer: AA/no BA	1.7 (.058)	1.8 (.065)	0.9 (.035)	1.3 (.058)	1.7 (.072)	1.7 (.087)
Terminal AA	5.7 (.099)	5.9 (.106)	3.7 (.180)	6.7 (.436)	5.1 (.112)	6.4 (.145)
No degree, non-incidental 2- and 4-year	2.7 (.050)	2.5 (.049)	3.0 (.228)	5.0 (.414)	2.8 (.074)	2.5 (.079)
No degree, non-incidental 2-year only	15.6 (.217)	14.9 (.215)	18.3 (.688)	26.9 (.859)	15.8 (.192)	15.5 (.348)
No degree, incidental 2-year	7.6 (.098)	7.1 (.105)	10.8 (.281)	12.7 (.287)	7.3 (.124)	7.9 (.163)
No 2-year, but 4-year	49.3 (.331)	50.2 (.351)	47.8 (.714)	30.8 (1.027)	50.7 (.356)	47.9 (.432)
No 2- or 4-year, but proprietary/vocational	6.7 (.138)	6.5 (.149)	8.5 (.394)	8.0 (.384)	5.6 (.169)	7.8 (.196)
Other pattern	4.1 (.065)	4.2 (.069)	3.1 (.148)	3.6 (.498)	3.6 (.077)	4.9 (.075)

NOTE: The universe = all students whose records show any earned credits. N=12,332. Standard errors are in parentheses. Columns may not add to 100 due to rounding.

SOURCE: U.S. Department of Education, National Center for Education Statistics, NLS–72 Special Analysis Files.

Table 2.—Basic general postsecondary attendance patterns, by demographic group

	2/4 year transfer w/BA	2-year AA only	Non-incidental 2/4 year no degree	Vocational or incidental no degree	4-year only or other w/BA	4-year only or other no BA	No post-secondary
All	3.7%	4.2%	10.1%	7.8%	19.1%	11.3%	43.9%
	(.054)	(.059)	(.119)	(.088)	(.142)	(.108)	(.169)
SES							
Low	1.8	3.1	8.4	8.4	7.4	8.2	62.6
(25.0%)	(.052)	(.082)	(.217)	(.158)	(.182)	(.158)	(.296)
Medium	3.6	4.6	10.8	8.5	15.0	11.2	46.4
(50.1%)	(.095)	(.103)	(.122)	(.112)	(.184)	(.117)	(.220)
High	6.1	4.5	10.5	5.7	39.5	15.4	18.2
(24.9%)	(.113)	(.125)	(.268)	(.130)	(.304)	(.236)	(.252)
Race/ethnicity							
White/Asian	4.0	4.4	9.9	7.6	20.6	11.2	42.3
(86.0%)	(.057)	(.067)	(.121)	(.096)	(.160)	(.114)	(.181)
Black	1.8	2.2	10.0	9.1	11.1	13.8	52.1
(9.6%)	(.095)	(.086)	(.392)	(.220)	(.304)	(.316)	(.498)
Hisp/American	2.3	3.5	13.8	9.1	6.7	8.9	55.8
Indian (4.4%)	(.217)	(.218)	(.419)	(.246)	(.407)	(.374)	(.612)
Sex							
Men	4.3	3.9	10.7	7.7	20.1	11.7	41.4
(50.0%)	(.081)	(.080)	(.125)	(.113)	(.213)	(.123)	(.274)
Women	3.1	4.4	9.5	7.8	18.0	10.9	46.3
(50.0%)	(.058)	(.083)	(.174)	(.114)	(.198)	(.154)	(.224)
Parents' language							
Non-English-	4.0	3.6	11.2	7.9	18.1	12.8	42.5
speaking	(.178)	(.093)	(.461)	(.361)	(.439)	(.361)	(.527)
(6.9%)							
English-	3.7	4.2	10.0	7.8	19.1	11.2	44.0
speaking	(.052)	(.063)	(.113)	(.086)	(.146)	(.107)	(.168)

NOTE: The universe = all NLS–72 participants. N=22,652. Standard errors in parentheses. Rows may not add to 100 due to rounding.

SOURCE: U.S. Department of Education, National Center for Education Statistics, NLS–72 Special Analysis Files.

Table 3.—SES and community college attendance through 1984

	SES		
	Lowest quartile	Middle two quartiles	Highest quartile
Total NLS/PETS	17.7%	47.1%	35.2%
Never attended CC	15.8	43.9	40.3
All CC attendees	19.5	51.6	28.8
All black CC attendees	**56.3**	**36.4**	**7.3**
[All blacks in PETS	54.0	37.4	8.6]
All Hispanic CC attendees	**51.3**	**39.1**	**9.6**
[All Hispanics in PETS	53.2	36.7	10.1]
All white CC attendees	**14.0**	**53.9**	**32.1**
[All whites in PETS	12.6	48.5	38.9]
By pattern of community college attendance:			
Transfer, AA + BA	11.4	49.3	39.3
Transfer, BA/no AA	14.6	46.1	39.3
Transfer, AA/no BA	10.7	51.8	37.5
Terminal AA	21.3	55.5	23.2
No degree, non-incidental 2- and 4-year	14.6	44.0	41.4
No degree, non-incidental 2-year only	22.6	54.3	23.1
No degree, incidental 2-year	25.9	53.3	20.9
No 2-, but 4-year	13.8	42.1	44.1
No 2- or 4-year, but proprietary/vocational	32.8	53.1	14.1
Other pattern	9.1	43.2	47.7

NOTE: The universe = all students for whom at least one postsecondary transcript was received. N=12,599. Rows may not add to 100 due to rounding.

SOURCE: U.S. Department of Education, National Center for Education Statistics, NLS–72 Special Analysis Files.

Table 4.—Students from non-English-speaking households in NLS/PETS

Percent of NLS/PETS students, by racial/ethnic group, who come from non-English-speaking households:

Hispanic/American Indian	34.8%
Black	6.2
White/Asian/other	6.0
All	7.1

Percent of NLS/PETS students from non-English-speaking households who are:

Hispanic/American Indian	17.9%
Black	7.5
White/Asian/other	74.6

Percent of NLS/PETS students, by community college attendance pattern (columns add to 100)	**From non-English-speaking**	**From English-speaking**
Transfer,.AA + BA	3.1 (.167)	3.3 (.070)
Transfer, BA but no AA	3.9 (.254)	3.2 (.070)
Transfer, AA but no BA	1.8 (.030)	1.7 (.064)
Terminal AA	4.6 (.169)	5.7 (.110)
No degree, non-incidental 2- and 4-year	3.0 (.192)	2.7 (.054)
No degree, non-incidental 2-year only	17.1 (.718)	15.7 (.216)
No degree, incidental 2-year	8.0 (.420)	7.5 (.104)
No 2-year, but 4-year	48.1 (.787)	49.4 (.323)
No 2- or 4-year, but proprietary/vocational	5.2 (.469)	6.8 (.128)
Other pattern	5.2 (.439)	4.0 (.062)

NOTE: The universe = all NLS/PETS students whose postsecondary transcripts show any earned credits. N=12,332. Standard errors are in parentheses.

SOURCE: U.S. Department of Education, National Center for Education Statistics, NLS–72 Special Analysis Files.

Table 5.—Age in last year of attendance at a community college, by sex

Age	All	Men	Women
18 (1972)	4.6%	5.0%	4.1%
19 (1973)	14.0	12.8	15.3
20 (1974)	21.7	23.5	19.9
21 (1975)	10.1	10.8	9.5
22 (1976)	8.2	8.5	7.8
23/24 (1977–78)	14.9	14.8	14.9
25/26 (1979–80)	11.8	10.9	12.7
27-30 (1981–84)	14.8	13.8	15.8

NOTE: The universe = all students who attended community colleges and whose community college transcripts included complete term date information. N=5,485. Columns may not add to 100 due to rounding.

SOURCE: U.S. Department of Education, National Center for Education Statistics, NLS–72 Special Analysis Files.

Table 6.—Time between first and last enrollment in community colleges through 1984, by community college attendance pattern

CC attendance pattern	Months between first and last enrollment						
	<6	6-15	16-27	28-39	40-65	66-99	100+
				(percent)			
% of all time periods	**26.7%**	**20.6%**	**16.6%**	**8.5%**	**10.8%**	**10.1%**	**6.7%**
Transfer, AA+BA	0.7	32.7	33.0	10.1	8.7	10.9	3.9
Transfer, BA but no AA	20.8	29.3	20.3	8.3	8.6	8.2	4.6
Transfer, AA but no BA	0.8	24.9	28.1	10.4	14.5	12.8	8.4
Terminal AA	2.1	21.5	23.4	13.0	13.6	14.8	11.6
No degree, non-incidental 2- and 4-year	21.1	18.2	20.5	9.4	12.0	11.4	7.5
No degree, non-incidental 2-year only	21.4	20.9	13.8	9.2	13.2	12.6	8.9
No degree, incidental 2-year	61.0	14.0	7.8	4.0	5.8	4.6	2.7
Other pattern	59.1	12.9	10.5	5.0	7.5	3.6	1.4

NOTE: The universe = all students who attended at least one community college and whose community college transcripts included complete term date information. N=5,485. Rows may not add to 100 due to rounding.

SOURCE: U.S. Department of Education, National Center for Education Statistics, NLS–72 Special Analysis Files.

Table 7.—Delayed entry to postsecondary education by community college attendance pattern

Attendance pattern	% of CC attendees	Delayed entry (in months)				
		No Delay	7-18	19-30	31-54	55+
All		**72.5%**	**9.6%**	**5.0%**	**6.5%**	**6.5%**
Transfer, AA + BA	**7.6**	87.9	7.0	2.4	2.7	0.0
Transfer, BA/no AA	**7.4**	86.2	8.9	2.8	2.1	0.1
Transfer, AA/no BA	**3.9**	88.8	6.4	4.1	0.7	0.0
Terminal AA	**13.1**	70.8	10.5	5.3	6.9	6.4
No degree, non-incidental 2- and 4-year	**6.0**	84.0	10.0	3.0	2.9	0.2
No degree, non-incidental at 2-year only	**35.4**	60.7	12.9	6.9	10.2	9.4
No degree, incidental 2-year	**17.3**	34.0	16.8	10.5	17.9	20.9
No 2-year, but 4-year	—	80.9	7.3	3.8	3.9	4.1
No 2- or 4-year, but proprietary/vocational	—	50.6	14.2	7.2	13.0	15.0
Other pattern	**9.3**	85.8	6.4	3.9	2.7	1.2

— Not applicable.

NOTE: The universe = all students with known dates of entry to any postsecondary institution. N=12,279. Rows may not add to 100 due to rounding.

SOURCE: U.S. Department of Education, National Center for Education Statistics, NLS–72 Special Analysis Files.

Table 8.—Year of first attendance at a community college by community college attendance pattern

CC attendance pattern	1972	1973	1974	1975	1976	77-78	79-80	1981-4
All	**52.6%**	**14.7%**	**8.8%**	**5.6%**	**5.5%**	**7.7%**	**4.2%**	**0.8%**
Transfer, AA, then BA	80.7	9.7	4.3	4.1	1.3	0.0	0.0	0.0
Transfer, BA, no AA	71.1	17.5	6.7	2.1	2.3	0.4	0.0	0.0
Transfer, AA, no BA	55.6	17.4	10.6	4.6	5.0	3.7	3.2	0.0
Terminal AA	69.4	10.5	5.9	3.4	3.8	6.4	0.5	0.1
No degree, non-incidental 2- and 4-year	44.4	19.4	10.9	8.5	3.9	7.6	4.8	0.5
No degree, non-incident 2-year only	58.2	3.4	7.0	5.3	5.5	6.5	3.7	0.4
No degree, incidental 2-year	30.0	17.5	10.7	9.3	9.3	11.6	8.7	2.9
Other pattern	14.9	18.1	9.7	5.6	8.3	21.1	10.9	1.4

NOTE: The universe = at least one transcript received from a community college with complete term date information. N=5,485. Rows may not add to 100 due to rounding.

SOURCE: U.S. Department of Education, National Center for Education Statistics, NLS–72 Special Analysis Files.

Table 9.—Active military duty and community college attendance

Part I: General postsecondary attendance pattern, by race

	All	Hisp/American Indian (4.2%)	Black (14.6%)	White/Asian (81.1%)	All military
Transfer with BA	3.8%	6.7%	0.7%	2.6%	2.5%
Terminal AA	4.2	3.6	4.3	4.6	4.5
No degree, non-incidental 2/4-year or 2-year only	10.1	24.1	10.4	15.0	14.7
No degree, incidental 2-year or proprietary/vocational	7.8	11.0	15.0	9.7	10.5
No 2-year, but 4-year or other, with BA	19.1	5.8	4.6	10.0	9.0
No 2-year, but 4-year or other, no BA	11.5	7.8	9.5	10.9	10.6
No postsecondary	43.4	41.0	55.5	47.3	48.2

Part II: CC attendance pattern, by year of first CC attendance

	1972	1973	1974	1975	1976	1977-79	1980+
Transfer, AA + BA	18.8%	12.0%	28.9%	27.0%	13.4%	0.0%	0.0%
Transfer, BA no AA	47.3	22.5	0.0	20.5	9.7	0.0	0.0
Transfer/AA no BA	7.3	18.6	21.8	7.5	11.3	33.6	0.0
Terminal AA	22.6	9.6	7.2	13.7	16.2	29.8	1.0
No degree, 2- & 4-year, non-incidental	32.4	3.7	7.4	28.4	11.6	16.6	0.0
No degree, non-incidental 2-year only	31.7	7.2	6.6	8.7	18.0	25.0	2.9
No degree, incidental 2-year	20.0	8.6	14.1	7.1	12.2	36.9	1.1
Other pattern	16.7	19.4	16.2	1.7	7.0	38.9	0.0

NOTE: The universes: Part I=NLS–72 students who indicated active military duty between 1972 and 1979 (N=1,667). Part II=NLS/PETS students (transcript received) who were on active military duty at any time between 1972 and 1979 (N=867).

SOURCE: U.S. Department of Education, National Center for Education Statistics, NLS–72 Special Analysis Files.

Table 10.—Educational aspirations v. educational plans of NLS–72 students as seniors in high school

	Aspired to	Planned
All		
High school graduate	13.1% (.119)	23.9% (.148)
Postsecondary vocational	23.0 (.136)	20.6 (.149)
2-year college/Associate's	9.6 (.089)	12.4 (.110)
4-year college/Bachelor's	25.9 (.115)	30.6 (.148)
Graduate/professional school	28.5 (.164)	12.5 (.125)
Sex		
Women		
High school graduate	15.2 (.187)	27.4 (.250)
Postsecondary vocational	24.4 (.180)	21.0 (.180)
2-year college/Associate's	10.8 (.128)	13.2 (.161)
4-year college/Bachelor's	24.5 (.154)	29.1 (.204)
Graduate/professional school	25.1 (.235)	9.3 (.177)
Men		
High school graduate	11.1 (.139)	20.4 (.178)
Postsecondary vocational	21.5 (.199)	20.2 (.183)
2-year college/Associate's	8.3 (.113)	11.6 (.123)
4-year college/Bachelor's	27.2 (.175)	32.1 (.201)
Graduate/professional school	31.9 (.208)	15.7 (.151)
Race		
White/Asian		
High school graduate	13.2 (.132)	24.2 (.170)
Postsecondary vocational	22.2 (.147)	19.5 (.168)
2-year college/Associate's	9.5 (.092)	12.4 (.121)
4-year college/Bachelor's	26.2 (.131)	31.3 (.170)
Graduate/professional school	29.0 (.178)	12.6 (.139)
Black		
High school graduate	11.0 (.249)	19.0 (.341)
Postsecondary vocational	28.1 (.361)	28.4 (.342)
2-year college/Associate's	9.4 (.403)	11.1 (.384)
4-year college/Bachelor's	23.9 (.327)	27.8 (.306)
Graduate/professional school	27.6 (.353)	13.8 (.297)
Hispanic/American Indian		
High school graduate	17.4 (.458)	29.9 (.476)
Postsecondary vocational	27.6 (.464)	26.0 (.445)
2-year college/Associate's	12.1 (.318)	15.2 (.472)
4-year college/Bachelor's	23.7 (.481)	21.3 (.441)
Graduate/professional school	19.3 (.638)	7.6 (.425)
SES		
Lowest SES quartile		
High school graduate	20.6% (.203)	38.2% (.276)
Postsecondary vocational	32.9 (.234)	27.0 (.263)
2-year college/Associate's	9.9 (.203)	10.4 (.171)
4-year college/Bachelor's	20.1 (.201)	18.3 (.228)
Graduate/professional school	16.5 (.233)	6.2 (.147)

Table 10.—Educational aspirations v. educational plans of NLS–72 students as seniors in high school—Continued

	Aspired to		Planned	
Middle two SES quartiles				
High school graduate	14.1	(.158)	25.5	(.196)
Postsecondary vocational	24.9	(.205)	22.6	(.209)
2-Year college/Associate's	11.0	(.112)	14.2	(.170)
4-Year college/Bachelor's	25.2	(.174)	28.0	(.199)
Graduate/professional school	24.8	(.212)	9.7	(.130)
Highest SES quartile				
High school graduate	4.0	(.131)	7.2	(.169)
Postsecondary vocational	9.5	(.164)	10.5	(.170)
2-year college/Associate's	6.5	(.132)	10.6	(.189)
4-year college/Bachelor's	32.8	(.271)	47.6	(.293)
Graduate/professional school	47.3	(.306)	24.2	(.287)
SAT				
700 or Less				
High school graduate	7.3	(.277)	11.7	(.363)
Postsecondary vocational	18.7	(.487)	19.9	(.493)
2-year college/Associate's	13.1	(.378)	19.8	(.420)
4-year college/Bachelor's	35.4	(.490)	38.0	(.556)
Graduate/professional school	25.5	(.443)	10.6	(.339)
701–975				
High school graduate	3.1	(.138)	6.1	(.164)
Postsecondary vocational	10.2	(.171)	11.8	(.218)
2-year college/Associate's	8.2	(.184)	14.1	(.261)
4-year college/Bachelor's	40.0	(.402)	53.2	(.355)
Graduate/professional school	38.5	(.333)	14.8	(.197)
976–1148				
High school graduate	1.2	(.082)	2.3	(.166)
Postsecondary vocational	4.4	(.197)	5.3	(.206)
2-year college/Associate's	3.7	(.091)	7.2	(.275)
4-year college/Bachelor's	31.1	(.481)	59.8	(.522)
Graduate/professional school	59.6	(.536)	25.4	(.501)
Above 1148				
High school graduate	0.8	(.088)	1.6	(.108)
Postsecondary vocational	2.0	(.172)	2.3	(.217)
2-year college/Associate's	1.0	(.108)	2.6	(.131)
4-year college/Bachelor's	21.6	(.444)	47.0	(.513)
Graduate/professional school	74.6	(.472)	46.5	(.487)

NOTE: The universe = all NLS–72 students whose transcripts show any completed, non-transfer courses, and who answered questions on educational aspirations and plans in either the Base Year or Supplemental Survey. (N=21,106. For those with SAT/ACT scores, N=8,862.)

SOURCE: U.S. Department of Education, National Center for Education Statistics, NLS–72 Special Analysis Files.

Table 11.—Educational aspirations and plans in 1972 versus highest degrees actually earned by 1984

Aspirations/plans as high school seniors	Highest degree earned to 1984				
	None	Certificate	Associate's	Bachelor's	Graduate
High school diploma only					
Aspired	83.6%	4.6%	6.2%	4.5%	1.1%
Planned	78.1	7.0	7.8	6.4	0.6
Postsecondary vocational					
Aspired	66.0	16.6	11.6	5.4	0.3
Planned	65.5	17.4	11.2	5.4	0.6
Associate's degree					
Aspired	60.3	8.0	22.6	7.9	1.2
Planned	60.6	4.8	20.1	13.2	1.4
Bachelor's degree					
Aspired	46.0	2.4	9.3	37.8	4.5
Planned	36.4	1.4	6.4	47.3	8.5
Graduate degree					
Aspired	33.2	1.7	5.1	45.6	14.5
Planned	29.9	1.1	4.7	45.6	18.7

NOTE: The universe = all students who answered 1972 questions about their educational aspirations and plans. N=11,831. Rows may not add to 100 due to rounding.

SOURCE: U.S. Department of Education, National Center for Education Statistics, NLS–72 Special Analysis Files.

Table 12.—Community college attendance pattern by high school class rank

Attendance pattern	High school class rank in quintiles				
	High	2nd	3rd	4th	Low
Transfer, AA + BA	36.6% (1.02)	23.5% (.907)	20.1% (.736)	15.3% (.852)	4.3% (.237)
Transfer, BA/no AA	30.6 (.699)	27.6 (1.07)	23.9 (1.00)	14.0 (.811)	4.0 (.095)
Transfer, AA/no BA	23.4 (1.08)	28.7 (1.32)	22.0 (1.48)	15.8 (1.00)	9.7 (1.18)
Terminal AA from CC	20.1 (.624)	25.0 (.596)	26.7 (.599)	18.8 (.853)	9.3 (.285)
No degree, non-incidental, 2 and 4-year	23.1 (.907)	25.8 (1.00)	23.4 (.635)	19.2 (.847)	8.6 (.835)
No degree, non-incidental, 2-year only	13.9 (.360)	19.3 (.445)	25.3 (.425)	23.7 (.452)	17.9 (.445)
No degree, incidental 2-year	11.2 (.401)	18.9 (.575)	21.8 (.484)	26.9 (.535)	21.3 (.552)
No 2-year, but 4-year	40.7 (.302)	26.2 (.226)	17.6 (.216)	11.3 (.166)	4.3 (.124)
No 2- or 4-year, but proprietary/vocational	16.2 (.404)	19.6 (.713)	23.3 (.699)	25.1 (.810)	15.7 (.557)
Other pattern	40.1 (.769)	28.4 (.727)	17.6 (.628)	10.0 (.601)	3.9 (.445)
No postsecondary	9.0 (.131)	16.8 (.200)	22.5 (.177)	26.0 (.151)	25.6 (.191)

NOTE: The universe = all NLS–72 students for whom high school class rank could be computed. N=19,641. The N for those in the NLS/PETSsample who met this condition and earned any postsecondary credits is 11,017. Standard errors are in parentheses. Rows may not add to 100 due to rounding.

SOURCE: U.S. Department of Education, National Center for Education Statistics, NLS–72 Special Analysis Files.

Table 13.—High school curricula of the class of 1972 by general postsecondary attendance pattern through 1984

High school curricula	Number of semesters 0	1-2	3-4	5-6	7+
I. Foreign language					
All	48.4%	21.7%	18.6%	8.8%	2.5%
All PETS	34.8	24.7	24.6	12.4	3.5
Transfer with BA	28.0	29.2	30.1	9.4	3.3
Terminal AA from CC	36.5	26.9	23.2	11.0	2.4
No degree, non-incidental	44.1	27.8	20.7	6.5	0.8
No degree, trade/incidental	58.4	20.6	14.3	5.7	1.0
4-year/other with/BA	18.9	23.5	31.1	19.9	6.5
4-year/other no BA	32.2	26.1	25.4	12.7	3.6
No postsecondary	67.9	17.5	10.0	3.7	1.0
II. Science					
All	12.9	35.1	30.5	17.0	4.6
All PETS	9.5	28.9	33.2	22.2	6.3
Transfer with BA	5.7	26.1	34.7	25.7	7.8
Terminal AA from CC	10.8	31.1	32.1	20.7	5.4
No degree, non-incidental	11.8	37.2	32.9	14.6	3.6
No degree, trade/incidental	14.3	42.1	29.3	12.3	2.1
4-year/other, with/BA	6.8	18.0	33.7	31.7	9.8
4-year/other, no BA	8.4	26.7	35.8	22.4	6.8
No postsecondary	17.6	44.2	26.9	9.3	2.0
III. Math					
All	14.4	27.4	29.0	23.6	5.7
All PETS	9.8	22.1	29.9	30.4	7.9
Transfer with BA	5.4	18.9	34.9	32.8	7.9
Terminal AA from CC	11.4	25.8	32.3	24.2	6.3
No degree, non-incidental	11.7	28.4	32.7	22.5	4.8
No degree, trade/incidental	16.7	34.1	28.6	17.6	3.0
4-year/other, with/BA	6.5	11.6	27.1	43.0	11.8
4-year/other, no BA	8.4	21.4	31.2	30.5	8.6
No postsecondary	20.8	35.4	27.5	13.6	2.8
IV. Fine or performing arts					
All	58.6	17.3	9.9	7.9	6.3
All PETS	56.1	17.4	10.1	8.9	7.5
Transfer with BA	59.6	14.3	10.6	9.0	6.5
Terminal AA from CC	58.1	18.6	9.7	7.3	6.3
No degree, non-incidental	55.2	18.0	10.3	9.6	6.9
No degree, trade/incidental	57.6	18.9	10.5	8.1	5.0
4-year/other, with/BA	55.7	16.0	9.4	9.7	9.3
4-year/other, no BA	54.2	18.5	10.8	8.7	7.8
No Postsecondary Ed	62.0	17.2	9.7	6.5	4.6

Table 13.—High school curricula of the class of 1972 by general postsecondary attendance pattern through 1984—Continued

High school curricula	Number of semesters 0	1-2	3-4	5-6	7+
V. Business/office					
All	51.7%	22.1%	10.5%	5.8%	10.0%
All PETS	52.4	25.3	10.6	4.8	4.9
Transfer with BA	50.4	29.1	11.7	5.4	3.5
Terminal AA from CC	49.3	23.5	10.9	5.4	10.9
No degree, non-incidental	47.6	24.2	11.6	6.3	10.4
No degree, trade/incidental	48.1	21.3	13.0	6.2	11.4
4-year/other, with/BA	59.1	27.8	8.0	2.5	2.6
4-year/other, no BA	52.8	25.8	11.0	5.3	5.2
No postsecondary	50.0	17.5	10.7	7.2	14.7
VI. Trade/Industrial Arts					
All	77.7	7.9	5.4	4.0	5.1
All PETS	81.3	7.9	4.4	3.0	3.4
Transfer with BA	79.5	10.2	4.3	4.0	2.0
Terminal AA from CC	80.5	8.6	4.3	3.1	3.6
No degree, non-incidental	74.8	8.5	6.0	4.8	6.0
No degree, trade/incidental	72.3	9.6	6.1	5.0	7.0
4-year/other, with/BA	88.8	6.3	2.8	1.2	0.9
4-year/other, no BA	82.4	7.8	4.9	2.6	2.3
No postsecondary	72.8	7.8	6.5	5.2	7.7

NOTE: The universes: "All"=NLS–72 students for whom high school records were available (N=22,652); "All PETS"=(N=12,599). Rows may not add to 100 due to rounding.

SOURCE: U.S. Department of Education, National Center for Education Statistics, NLS–72 Special Analysis Files.

Table 14.—Equated 1972 SAT/ACT scores by highest degree earned to 1984, and by general postsecondary attendance pattern

	Mean	Standard deviation	Standard error	Min	Max	N
Part I: NLS–72	**934**	**207**	**2.162**	**474**	**1560**	**9,197**
By attendance						
Transfer with BA	919	188	7.827	490	1495	577
Terminal AA from CC	876	165	7.604	474	1424	469
No degree, non-incidental	842	169	5.544	474	1554	934
No degree, trade/incidental	838	173	7.961	474	1554	472
4-year/other, w/BA	1027	196	3.232	474	1560	3,662
4-year/other, no BA	913	197	4.941	474	1495	1,584
No postsecondary	836	198	5.123	474	1554	1,499
Part II: NLS/PETS	953	204	2.321	474	1560	7,698
By highest degree						
No degree	880	189	3.508	474	1554	2,893
AA degree	870	167	7.009	474	1424	565
BA degree	995	194	3.487	474	1560	3,080
BA+, no graduate degree	1008	197	10.538	474	1539	348
Master's	1046	196	8.154	506	1539	580
Ph.D./1st professional	1173	182	11.961	700	1539	232

NOTE: The universes: Part I=all NLS–72 students who took either the SAT or ACT (N=9,197). SAT/ACT scores are arrayed in 35 bands, from 474 to 1560; Part II=all NLS/PETS students who took either the SAT or ACT and earned any postsecondary credits, 1972-1984 (N=7,698).

SOURCE: U.S. Department of Education, National Center for Education Statistics, NLS–72 Special Analysis Files.

Table 15.—The fate of "high ability" students: SES, attendance patterns, and degree attainment to 1984

	All	Socioeconomic status in 1972: Lowest quartile	Mid two quartiles	Highest quartile
Part I, by attendance pattern				
Transfer with BA	4.6% (.231)	5.1% (1.13)	6.5% (.510)	3.2% (.149)
Terminal Associate's	2.9 (.208)	4.3 (.218)	3.8 (.386)	2.1 (.299)
No degree, non-incidental	3.5 (.238)	3.6 (2.46)	4.7 (.469)	2.6 (.205)
Proprietary or incidental	2.2 (.207)	2.2 (1.29)	3.2 (.448)	0.7 (.193)
4-year/other w/BA	64.3 (.551)	57.9 (2.73)	53.8 (1.20)	72.7 (.721)
4-year/other no BA	14.3 (.422)	14.2 (1.43)	16.1 (.788)	13.0 (.501)
No postsecondary	8.3 (.413)	12.8 (1.75)	11.0 (.818)	5.7 (.344)
Part II, by highest degree earned				
None	19.3 (.483)	18.5 (2.85)	23.8 (.890)	16.4 (.600)
Certificate/license	2.0 (.049)	2.6 (.134)	3.5 (.126)	0.8 (.017)
Associate's	3.9 (.342)	7.3 (1.43)	5.7 (.806)	2.3 (.310)
Bachelor's	51.2 (.543)	49.7 (2.70)	49.1 (1.04)	52.9 (.865)
Graduate	23.6 (.439)	22.0 (1.89)	17.9 (.838)	27.6 (.650)

NOTE: The universes: Part I=all NLS–72 students who (a) scored in the top quartile of the ability test given to them as high school seniors, (b) ranked in the top 25% of their high school graduating classes, and (c) took, in high school, either more than 5 semesters of math or more than 5 semesters of science or more than 5 semesters of foreign languages (N=1,117); Part II=all NLS/PETS students who met the same criteria as stated for universe I (N=1,020). Standard errors in parentheses. Columns may not add to 100 due to rounding.

SOURCE: U.S. Department of Education, National Center for Education Statistics, NLS–72 Special Analysis Files.

Table 16.—Community college "majors" of the NLS/PETS sample

"Major"	Associate's degree holders	No-degree group
"Liberal Arts & Sciences"*	21.2%	11.7%
General Studies	17.6	8.6
Nursing/Allied Health	13.1	3.5
Business Administration/Accounting	10.0	8.8
Office/Business Support	8.4	8.8
Engineering and Science Technology	6.9	5.2
Education/Human Services	4.5	2.2
Protective Services	4.0	2.6
Agriculture and Natural Resources	3.3	1.3
Fine and Performing Arts	3.3	3.4
Trades/Precision Production	2.8	6.5
Sciences	2.1	1.1
Computer Science/Data Processing	2.1	2.5
Indeterminable	0.8	34.1
Personal Services	0.1	0.1

*Includes both "general transfer" curricula (i.e., lower-division distribution of courses across all the traditional arts and sciences fields) and curricula emphasizing either humanities or social sciences.

NOTE: The universe = all students who either (a) received an Associate's Degree from a community college (N=1,342), or (b) earned more than 29 credits in community colleges but no degree of any kind (N=1,027).

SOURCE: U.S. Department of Education, National Center for Education Statistics, NLS–72 Special Analysis Files.

Table 17.—Course-taking differentials by community college attendance pattern*

Course	Ratio
Stenography	6.75
Secretarial: General	6.60
Office Machines	4.68
Technical Mathematics	4.19
Business Math: Arithmetic-Based	4.17
Nursing: General	2.93
Remedial Reading	2.86
Law Enforcement: General Police Training	2.78
Arithmetic	2.76
General Technical Drafting	2.65
Remedial English: General, Writing	2.58
Data Processing	2.50
Office Management/Supervision	2.35
Business Administration: General	2.27
Business English	2.23
Interpersonal Skills	2.14
Pre-Collegiate Algebra	2.07
Anatomy & Physiology	1.92
Freshman Orientation	1.91
Introduction to Accounting	1.75
Drawing	1.67
Self-Awareness, Human Potential	1.66
Social Sciences: General	1.65
Health Science and Services: General	1.64
Human Nutrition (Home Economics)	1.63

*The table answers the question: How much more likely were NLS/PETS students to take a particular course in an attendance pattern largely limited to community colleges (Community College Attendance Patterns #4-7) versus an attendance pattern involving both community colleges and 4-year colleges (Community College Attendance Patterns #1-3)? The answer is expressed in a ratio reflecting the fact that there are 2.86 times as many students in the first pattern as in the second.

NOTE: Only courses taken by 20% or more of the students are included. The 25 courses with the highest ratios are listed.

SOURCE: U.S. Department of Education, National Center for Education Statistics, NLS–72 Special Analysis Files.

Table 18.—Courses registering the highest percentage of credits earned, by community college attendance pattern

	Community college only	% of credits	Community college and 4-year	% of credits
1.	English Composition: Regular	5.2	English Composition: Regular	3.7
2.	General Psychology	3.0	General Biology	2.3
3.	General Biology	2.1	General Psychology	2.1
4.	Introduction to Accounting	2.1	Physical Education (Activities)	1.9
5.	Physical Education (Activities)	1.9	General Chemistry	1.8
6.	Introduction to Sociology	1.8	Introduction to Economics	1.7
7.	Introduction to Communications	1.6	Calculus	1.5
8.	Remedial English/Writing	1.5	Introduction to Sociology	1.5
9.	Nursing: General	1.5	World/Western Civilization	1.4
10.	Introduction to Economics	1.4	Introduction to Accounting	1.4
11.	General Chemistry	1.4	U.S. Government	1.3
12.	Stenography, Shorthand	1.3	Introduction to Physics	1.2
13.	World/Western Civilization	1.2	U.S. History Survey	1.1
14.	U.S. Government	1.2	Music Performance	1.1
15.	Pre-college Algebra	1.1	Introduction to Communication	1.1
16.	U.S. History: Survey	1.1	Advanced Accounting	1.1
17.	Secretarial: General	1.0	Elementary/Intermediate Spanish	1.0
18.	College Algebra	1.0	College Algebra	1.0
19.	Anatomy and Physiology	1.0	Introduction to Literature	0.8
20.	Automotive Mechanics	1.0	Business Law	0.8
21.	Introduction to Business	0.9	English Literature	0.8
22.	Business Law	0.9	Developmental Psychology	0.8
23.	Elementary/Intermediate Spanish	0.8	Art History	0.7
24.	Basic/Remedial Math	0.7	General Nursing	0.7
25.	Business Math: Arithmetic	0.7	Introduction to Management	0.7
26.	Calculus	0.7	American Literature	0.7
27.	Music Performance	0.7	Organic Chemistry	0.6
28.	Technical Mathematics	0.7	Statistics (Math)	0.6
29.	Introduction to Literature	0.7	Physical Science: General	0.6
30.	Clerk-Typist	0.7	Zoology: General	0.6
31.	Introduction to Physics	0.7	Philosophy: Introduction	0.6
32.	Remedial Reading	0.6	U.S. History Since 1865	0.6
33.	Data Processing	0.6	U.S. History to 1865	0.5
34.	Introduction to Management	0.6	Elementary/Intermediate French	0.5
35.	Health Activities: General	0.6	Physical Education (Education)	0.5
36.	Art History	0.6	Bible Studies	0.5
37.	U.S. History since 1865	0.6	Anatomy & Physiology	0.5
38.	Electronics Technology	0.6	Remedial English/Writing	0.5
39.	U.S. History to 1865	0.5	Basic Mathematics	0.5
40.	Advanced Accounting	0.5	Finance	0.5
41.	Nursing: Medical/Surgical	0.5	Pre-college Algebra	0.5
42.	Introduction to College-level Math	0.5	Geography: Introduction	0.5
43.	Computer Programming	0.5	Geology: General	0.5
	Total % of credits, top 43:	48.3		43.3

SOURCE: U.S. Department of Education, National Center for Education Statistics, NLS–72 Special Analysis Files.

Table 19.—Illustrative course enrollment differentials: Community colleges v. other types of postsecondary institutions*

Community college dominance			Contrasting case		
Course	% CC	N	Course	% CC	N
Landscaping	34.7	103	General Horticulture	19.0	137
American Studies	26.9	799	Latin American Studies	11.6	181
Hispanic-American Studies	26.9	271	Afro-American Studies	11.0	589
Business Adminstration: General	49.1	1,568	Management: General	19.2	2,460
Business Law	30.1	2,674	Corporate Finance	5.9	1,621
Introduction to Accounting	37.8	5,325	Tax Accounting	13.3	952
Real Estate	31.3	729	Insurance	13.2	364
Retailing	43.8	400	General Marketing	19.0	1,072
Introduction to Communications	35.0	4,197	Mass Communications	9.2	619
Data Processing	56.2	978	Introduction to Computer Science	17.2	857
Engineering Physics	42.3	274	Engineering Mechanics	8.9	920
Occupational Therapy	26.3	160	Exercise Physiology	7.0	584
Nursing: General	31.4	2,139	Public Health Nursing	6.5	278
Child Development/Care	30.6	960	Family Relations	18.8	517
Technical Writing	32.5	840	Creative Writing	16.6	692
Anatomy and Physiology	37.7	1,773	Physiology: Human/Animal	8.0	1,052
Pre-college Algebra	59.4	2,034	Statistics (Math)	13.3	2,251
Philosophy: Introduction	23.9	2,002	Ethics	11.6	864
Physical Science: General	28.4	1,737	Geology: General	13.6	2,098
General Psychology	33.8	8,151	Developmental Psychology	16.0	2,556
Physical Anthropology	31.3	367	Anthropology: General	11.2	1,569
U.S. History: Survey	34.5	3,220	European History from 1789	7.3	589
Sociology: Deviance, etc.	23.9	1,395	Sociology: Race, Ethnic	15.5	465
Ceramics	29.8	607	Sculpture	16.9	325
Photography	34.4	934	Film Arts: General	17.4	391

*Some 22% of the 485,000 course enrollments for the 12,332 NLS/PETS students who earned any credits were in community colleges. This chart provides answers to the question: In which courses typically offered by both 2-year and 4-year institutions were enrollments dominated by community colleges? In other words, where was the community college the principal provider of knowledge to this cohort? The fields chosen are illustrative, not exhaustive, and, in each case, data are provided for a related course in which the percentage of enrollments in community colleges was comparatively low. Only courses taken by 1.0% or more of the students are included.

NOTE: Examples are presented in the order in which general fields (e.g., Agriculture, Allied Health, Home Economics, English) are presented in the Classification of Instructional Programs (CIP).

SOURCE: U.S. Department of Education, National Center for Education Statistics, NLS–72 Special Analysis Files.

Table 20.—Occupations in 1986 for community college attendees, by highest degree earned to 1984

Occupations	Earned no degree	Associate's degree	AA plus BA or higher degree
Managers/administrators	16.5%	13.0%	18.1%
Nurses & health technicians	3.0	13.0	6.1
Office support occupations	14.9	10.8	4.0
Teachers	0.5	1.7	16.1
Engineering technologies, other technical	6.1	11.3	8.3
Computer-related	1.5	2.8	3.7
Craftsmen	14.4	7.1	4.0
"Buy/sell," i.e., purchasers and salespeople	5.8	8.5	6.4
Other clerical	6.6	5.6	3.3
Operatives	7.4	4.4	0.9
Other	23.3	21.8	29.1

NOTE: The universe = all students who earned any credits from a community college through 1984, who participated in the fifth (1986) followup survey, and who indicated a current (February 1986) occupation. N=2,927. Columns may not add to 100 due to rounding.

SOURCE: U. S. Dept. of Education, National Center for Education Statistics, NLS–72 Special Analysis Files.

Table 21.—The emphases of work in 1986 for NLS/PETS students who received Associate's degrees from community colleges, by community college "major"

Community college "major":	In most recent job, worked "a great deal with"	
	Ideas	People
All:	**50.1%**	**71.5%**
Agriculture, natural resources	48.8	56.4
Engineering technician/other technical	64.8	68.5
Business	49.6	78.4
Business support services	43.7	67.5
Computer science	59.4	59.7
Education/human services	28.5	48.8
Health/nursing	46.4	82.7
Miscellaneous trades	40.2	60.5
Protective services	57.2	87.3
Fine arts	58.0	85.2
Sciences	58.1	70.0
Liberal arts	53.3	74.7
General studies	54.1	67.7
Other	24.9	80.0
All of the above who also said they used their education "a great deal" on the job:	**70.1%**	**79.5%**
All BA recipients who never attended a community college:	**63.4%**	**79.5%**

NOTE: The universe = all students who received an Associate's degree from a community college, who participated in the fifth (1986) followup survey, and who indicated an occupation for 1985. N=914.

SOURCE: U.S. Department of Education, National Center for Education Statistics, NLS–72 Special Analysis Files.

Table 22.—General postsecondary attendance pattern and selected jobs at thirtysomething

Occupational areas	College attendance pattern					
	No post-secondary	4-year only/ other	Trans-fer w/BA	Terminal AA from CC	Both types, 2/4 year	Vocational or incidental
Business						
Accountant	0.7%	4.5%	4.8%	1.1%	1.1%	2.0%
Bookkeeper	2.2	0.7	0.4	1.0	2.2	0.7
Personnel Worker	0.2	1.2	5.4	0.4	0.4	0.9
Secretary	5.7	2.2	1.4	6.3	5.0	6.7
Sales: Wholesale	0.6	0.9	1.2	1.8	2.2	0.2
Sales: Manufacturing/ Construction	0.6	1.2	2.2	1.4	1.7	0.5
Manager: Financial Services	1.2	2.6	3.5	0.5	1.5	1.2
Manager: Sales	3.4	4.3	3.2	3.8	7.3	3.0
Manager: Manufacturing	1.8	2.7	2.2	2.6	1.6	1.3
Manager: Human Services	1.2	2.0	3.1	1.4	0.6	1.1
Science/Engineering/Technical						
Computer Programmer	0.1	2.5	1.9	1.6	1.1	1.1
Other Computer Specialist	0.4	1.0	2.2	1.5	0.9	0.5
Computer Equipment Operator	1.5	1.2	0.1	1.6	1.0	1.6
Engineer	0.0	3.5	4.6	0.0	0.0	0.2
Electronic Technician	0.6	0.6	0.7	7.0	2.0	1.9
Engineering/Sciences Technician	2.0	1.0	0.2	2.4	2.0	2.1
Health Services						
Nurses	0.4	2.7	1.7	7.0	1.8	2.4
Health Technician	1.0	2.7	1.8	4.5	1.5	1.5
Health Support	1.6	0.5	0.3	1.4	2.4	1.4
Doctors/Dentists	0.0	2.4	0.5	0.0	0.0	0.1
Production/Operation						
Carpenter	1.5	0.5	0.6	0.4	1.6	1.3
Machinist/Mechanic	4.9	1.1	0.3	1.8	4.5	6.1
Bus/Truck Driver	3.0	0.4	0.0	0.6	1.0	2.1
Production Control	0.5	0.4	0.1	0.7	2.2	0.4
Human Services						
Lawyer	0.0	2.0	1.2	0.0	0.0	0.1
Social Worker	0.2	1.1	2.2	0.7	0.4	0.2
School Teachers	0.0	3.3	5.9	0.0	0.0	0.0
Police	0.5	0.9	1.9	1.4	1.9	0.8
Other:	64.2	49.9	46.4	47.1	52.1	58.6

NOTE: The universe = all NLS students in the fifth (1986) followup survey, who indicated an occupation and earnings for 1985 and at least one full-time job between 10/79 and 2/86. N=8,623. Columns may not add to 100 due to rounding.

SOURCE: U.S. Department of Education, National Center for Education Statistics, NLS–72 Special Analysis Files.

Table 23.—Occupational aspirations at age 19 versus actual occupations at age 32

Occupation	I: Community college students				II: 4-year college students				III: No college	
	No degree (62.6%)		Degree (37.4%)		No degree (26.8%)		Degree (73.2%)			
	Plan	Real	Plan	Real	Plan	Real	Plan	Real	Plan	Real
Clerical	12.9%	20.0%	9.4%	16.6%	5.8%	17.5%	1.5%	8.0%	14.%	16.8%
Craftsmen	6.9	12.6	6.9	7.9	4.3	7.6	1.0	3.2	12.9	14.2
Operatives	2.0	6.5	0.4	3.6	0.8	4.4	0.1	0.8	6.0	12.5
Laborers	1.4	2.5	0.7	1.8	0.2	2.9	0.3	0.6	4.9	7.1
Homemakers[1]	10.6	12.1	9.1	13.8	8.2	13.8	3.6	9.5	23.1	18.9
(students	—	0.7	—	0.5	—	0.9	—	0.8	—	0.7)
"Managers"	10.2	13.2	10.7	10.4	11.6	15.5	9.1	16.9	7.7	9.8
Buy/sell[2]	2.3	5.8	1.9	5.2	1.6	6.7	0.8	5.0	2.0	3.9
Professional I[3]	21.9	12.2	26.6	21.5	29.8	17.3	35.0	23.3	10.6	6.0
Professional II[4]	8.5	0.7	7.4	3.7	15.6	1.7	25.4	12.5	2.1	0.5
Professional III (schoolteachers)	6.7	1.1	7.6	1.3	11.7	1.9	17.6	12.1	1.4	0.7
Technical	7.9	3.0	9.9	3.7	5.8	3.1	2.4	4.0	5.4	0.9
Other	8.6	10.3	9.4	10.5	4.7	7.6	3.3	4.1	8.9	8.7

—Not applicable.

[1] Includes full-time homemakers, full-time homemakers who were also students in 1986, and others.

[2] The 1973 category was "sales" only, and included insurance agents. In 1986, insurance agents are with stockbrokers in Professional I.

[3] A 1973 survey category, including accountant, artist, nurse, engineer, librarian, writer, social worker, actor, and athlete. In the 1986 categories, librarians/archivists are in Professional II.

[4] A 1973 category, including clergy, physician, lawyer, scientist, and college professor. In the 1986 categories, scientists are in Professional I.

NOTE: The universes: I=students who earned >10 credits from community colleges, did not earn a Bachelor's degree, answered the question "What kind of work will you be doing when you are 30 years old?" in the first followup survey in 1973, and participated in the fifth followup survey in 1986 (N=1,592); II= students who never attended a community college, earned >10 credits from a 4-year college, answered the 1973 question, and participated in the 1986 survey (N=3,846); III=students who did not attend college, answered the same question in 1973, and participated in the 1986 survey (N=3,935).

SOURCE: U.S. Department of Education, National Center for Education Statistics, NLS–72 Special Analysis Files.

Table 24.—Average earnings in current job, 1985, by community college attendance pattern

	All	Men	Women* without children	Women* with children
All	$21,184 (.008)	$25,022 (.010)	$18,970 (.018)	$15,016 (.017)
Transfer, AA + BA	21,862 (.038)	25,418 (.439)	17,892 (.075)	16,559 (.099)
Transfer, BA, no AA	22,827 (.036)	24,870 (.454)	22,049 (.084)	17,753 (.066)
Transfer, AA, no BA	19,795 (.057)	21,352 (.072)	19,180 (.106)	14,574 (.145)
Terminal AA	17,795 (.039)	22,139 (.048)	16,749 (.072)	12,449 (.076)
No degree, non-incidental 2- and 4-year	21,316 (.052)	26,513 (.052)	11,936 (.122)	13,286 (.113)
No degree, non-incidental 2-year only	19,982 (.024)	23,732 (.029)	17,769 (.061)	14,382 (.042)
No degree, incidental 2-year	18,030 (.035)	22,308 (.047)	12,782 (.086)	14,690 (.047)
No 2-year, but 4-Year	22,713 (.011)	26,508 (.013)	20,632 (.023)	15,881 (.025)
No 2- or 4-year, but proprietary/vocational	17,084 (.043)	19,982 (.051)	18,150 (.073)	11,911 (.095)
Other pattern	21,536 (.043)	26,919 (.053)	18,509 (.082)	16,112 (.092)

* For a full discussion of the rationale and consequences of analyzing women's earnings in these two groups, see *Women at Thirtysomething: Paradoxes of Attainment* (Adelman, 1991), in this series of monographs.

NOTE: The universe = all students whose transcripts show any earned credits, who also participated in the fifth (1986) followup survey, and indicated an occupation and earnings for 1985 and at least one full-time job between 10/79 and 2/86. N=5,864. Standard errors (in parentheses) refer to the log of the dollar figure.

SOURCE: U.S. Department of Education, National Center for Education Statistics, NLS–72 Special Analysis Files.

Table 25.—SES, general postsecondary attendance pattern, and home ownership at age 32

Attendance pattern	Percent owning home in 1986, by SES in 1972			
	All	Low SES (15.6%)	Medium SES (47.6%)	High SES (36.7%)
All	**63.3%** (0.240)	**59.6%** (0.514)	**64.6%** (0.330)	**64.3%** (0.489)
Transferred, earned BA	64.6 (0.587)	45.2 (1.418)	68.5 (0.897)	65.8 (0.965)
Terminal AA, including transfers, no BA	59.6 (0.653)	64.5 (1.764)	59.9 (0.797)	55.4 (1.644)
No degree: Non-incidental 2- and 4-year, or 2-year only	64.2 (1.162)	60.4 (1.681)	66.4 (0.737)	62.8 (1.048)
Incidental 2-year or no 2- or 4-year,[1] no degree	63.0 (3.726)	57.1 (0.629)	68.6 (1.460)	56.5 (0.894)
4-year only or other, earned BA[2]	67.7 (0.379)	62.0 (0.978)	67.0 (0.496)	69.4 (0.570)
4-year only or other, no BA[2]	59.7 (0.484)	62.5 (1.130)	61.8 (0.696)	55.4 (0.794)
No postsecondary	62.3 (0.471)	59.1 (0.735)	63.9 (0.669)	65.4 (.683)

[1] PETS students attending neither 2-year nor 4-year colleges attended proprietary vocational schools, Area Vocational-Technical Institutes, or specialized institutions such as hospital schools of nursing, radiology, etc.
[2] Most students in the "Other" attendance patterns either received their Associate's degrees from 4-year colleges or attended a community college after earning the Bachelor's.

NOTE: The universe = all students for whom socioeconomic status could be computed in 1972, and who participated in the fifth (1986) followup survey. N=12,682. Standard errors are in parentheses.

SOURCE: U.S. Department of Education, National Center for Education Statistics, NLS–72 Special Analysis Files.

13

Table 26.—Community college attendance and economic mobility

1972 SES and college attendance	1986 economic indicators		
	Mean 1985 earnings	Mean years job experience 10/76-2/86	Mean years of unemployment 10/76-2/86
Low SES (24.6%)	$15,440 (.013)	7.4 (.043)	0.84 (.030)
No postsecondary	14,138 (.018)	7.2 (.063)	0.98 (.045)
Vocational school or incidental 2-year	14,913 (.049)	7.9 (.139)	0.68 (.099)
No degree, both types, 2/4 year	16,904 (.050)	7.5 (.130)	0.80 (.096)
Terminal AA from community college	15,609 (.075)	7.9 (.194)	0.65 (.126)
Transfer with BA	17,845 (.068)	7.1 (.235)	0.78 (.138)
4-year only/other, w/BA	21,390 (.034)	7.7 (.088)	0.37 (.047)
4-year only/other, no BA	18,435 (.038)	7.9 (.113)	0.53 (.071)
Medium SES (47.7%)	18,191 (.013)	7.6 (.029)	0.68 (.018)
No postsecondary	16,225 (.018)	7.3 (.054)	0.87 (.036)
Vocational school or incidental 2-year	16,902 (.037)	8.0 (.095)	0.68 (.069)
No degree, both types, 2/4 year	20,145 (.030)	8.1 (.074)	0.59 (.050)
Terminal AA from community college	18,072 (.041)	7.8 (.134)	0.71 (.080)
Transfer with BA	21,003 (.041)	7.9 (.089)	0.43 (.049)
4-year only/other, w/BA	22,763 (.018)	7.7 (.052)	0.43 (.028)
4-year only/other, no BA	18,448 (.030)	8.1 (.079)	0.48 (.045)
High SES (27.8%)	22,051 (.013)	7.7 (.033)	0.54 (.021)
No postsecondary	18,998 (.040)	7.8 (.109)	0.66 (.068)
Vocational school or incidental 2-year	20,686 (.069)	7.5 (.170)	0.52 (.113)
No degree, both types, 2/4 year	21,059 (.042)	8.0 (.109)	0.56 (.073)
Terminal AA from community college	18,785 (.067)	7.7 (.173)	0.63 (.110)
Transfer with BA	24,433 (.039)	7.6 (.103)	0.42 (.067)
4-year only/other, w/BA	25,014 (.019)	7.7 (.045)	0.48 (.025)
4-year only/other, no BA	18,975 (.038)	7.7 (.088)	0.61 (.062)

NOTE: The universe = all NLS students for whom socioeconomic status in the base year (1972) or first followup (1973) could be determined, who also participated in the fifth (1986) followup and indicated both an occupation and earnings for 1985. N=9,265. Standard errors are in parentheses. Standard errors for earnings refer to the log of the dollar figure.

SOURCE: U.S. Department of Education, National Center for Education Statistics, NLS–72 Special Analysis Files.

☆ U.S. GOVERNMENT PRINTING OFFICE:1992-311-989/53064